More praise for *When Millennials Take Over*

Because Millennials are entering the workforce at an extraordinary time when our world is rapidly becoming more complex and connected, they will have a huge impact in how organizations are led and managed. That makes the impressive, actionable insights in *When Millennials Take Over* a must read for us all.

> -Kare Anderson, TED speaker on Opportunity Makers,
> author of *Mutuality Matters* and *Forbes* columnist

In this work, Jamie and Maddie share their insights into what makes successful modern organizations work, going beyond cliché and into the hard facts that will help leaders strengthen their culture across generational lines. Their focus on values is particularly critical for all leaders to master. Follow their guidance and build a culture that will unify your employees and place the power of transparent and diverse thinking squarely into your vision, mission and strategy.

> -Amith Nagarajan, Chairman and CEO, Aptify

When Millennials Take Over is critical reading for anyone who wants to understand the divide in expectations between the entrenched workforce and the next generation of management. Maddie and Jamie provide a well researched, insightful and thought provoking exploration into what it might take to bridge the gap between current work modalities and future norms and behavior patterns.

> -Ari Lightman, Professor, Digital Media and Marketing,
> Carnegie Mellon University

To succeed in the Millennial Age, businesses of all sizes must become fluent in social technology and learn to pivot in the face of constantly shifting customer expectations and industry changes. As a CEO (and Millennial), I highly recommend this book for any leader that wants to stay ahead of the curve—and consistently attract the best employees and most loyal customers.

> -Shama Hyder, CEO of The Marketing Zen Group and author,
> *The Zen of Social Media Marketing*

It's really refreshing to see an optimistic view of Millennials in the work-force! This book is a timely guide for any leader involved in technology and mobility, culture, and how organizations can prepare to meet the rapidly evolving expectations of employees.

-Daniel Kraft, President and CEO, Sitrion

Social business goes so much deeper than the technology. When *Millennials Take Over* shows us just how deep it goes. Read this book to understand how your company can thrive in the decades to come.

-Sandy Carter, leading social business executive

Want to view the world through the eyes of the Millennial generation? This is the book to read! Notter and Grant make a powerful case that we are in a revolutionary moment in history with major changes taking place in business, leadership, and management. They not only illustrate beautifully, with many fascinating case studies, the characteristics of this revolution, but they also offer practical advice on how to join. They demonstrate clearly that this revolution is already naturally embraced by the Millennial generation. The rest of us can either learn to understand this world and partner with the Millennials, or feel lost at sea.

-Hugh O'Doherty, Senior Associate at Cambridge Leadership Associates and Lecturer, John F. Kennedy School of Government

When I have the opportunity to speak in front of an audience of CEOs, I typically hear comments such as, "We don't really need to worry about how Millennials buy because our audiences are Baby Boomers." When *Millennials Take Over*, by Jamie Notter and Maddie Grant, shows not only that this thinking is wrong, but that this generation is the future of your business. They give you steps to prepare for a world when Millennials will be the decision-makers. The future is now.

-Gini Dietrich, CEO of Arment Dietrich and author of *Spin Sucks*

A scholarly yet eminently clear and accessible analysis on what Millennials–and all future workers–expect in today's workplace, and how to optimize your organization to meet those needs and truly engage the 21st century worker.

-Robert Berkman, Faculty, School of Media Studies,
the New School for Public Engagement and author of *Find it Fast: Extracting Expert Information from Social Networks, Big Data, Tweets, and More*

The Millennials are taking over–and depending on where you're standing, that's either really scary or the best news you've heard in a long time. Drawing on a wealth of research and illuminating case studies, Notter and Grant's book is a manifesto of change for the better. I'm ridiculously optimistic about the future. Read this book. You will be, too.

-Ted Coiné, CRO of Meddle.it and co-author, *A World Gone Social*

In *When Millennials Take Over*, Notter and Grant present a concise and thought-provoking look at how their research says management must change and why Millennials are the decoder rings for making this happen. As they did in *Humanize*, this book provides a roadmap to reach the goals they've identified for organizations: Digital. Clear. Fluid. Fast. Many of my clients will benefit from this book as soon as I can share it with them. Organizations do need to adapt and adopt. This book gives them some great ideas about how they can do that.

-Rick Rice, CEO RTR Communications

IDEAPRESS
PUBLISHING

When Millennials Take Over

Preparing for the Ridiculously Optimistic
Future of Business

Jamie Notter | Maddie Grant

IDEAPRESS
PUBLISHING

IDEAPRESS
PUBLISHING

Dedication

To the Fogdirockstars and the Boondogglers (you know who you are).
Thank you for teaching us what community really means.

And to Bo, Jackson, Sophie, Leah, and Taylor
— who will inherit this future of business, so let's make it a good one.

CONTENTS:

FOREWORD

It's true, you know. They will take over. Millennials will one day be in charge. And this is no thinly veiled hyperbolic threat. Rather, it's very simply a reality rooted in Workforce 101. Just as my generation (X) is finally grasping its just due reins, the newest generation to enter the workforce will one day do the same. And one day the generation already being dubbed as the "iGeneration," the "Homeland Generation," the "Plurals," and "Generation Z" will do exactly the same thing. Ad infinitum.

Accept this, Corporate Global. Accept it.

For once you do, we can all start getting down to what's really important – and potentially very powerful – about this whole generational dissonance. If we can find a way to heighten our awareness around the unique and distinct aspirations, motivators, and attractors for any generation, we can actually get down to creating the workplace, the culture, and the operating systems in which that generation will flourish. Intuitive? Maybe. But guess what: we've never (really) done this before. We've never (really) cared. We've haughtily protected and even blindly perpetuated the workplaces – the stuff, the actions, values, behaviors, beliefs - we've been taught to accept since the industrial revolution.

Okay, maybe *that's* a bit of hyperbole. But I have spent almost 25 years as a Human Resources leader and executive for some of the world's most formidable companies, and never have I seen a generation been so discerning about where they go to work. Never has one questioned – nay rejected – the norms to which we've all fallen prey. Never has one asked "why?" so much. Never has one openly chuckled at the inane, and then just gone about fixing it themselves. Millennials have increasingly demonstrated they are much more interested in understanding and appreciating *who* it is they are going to work with than they are concerned about *what* they'll do once they get there. They are looking for an experience beyond what will eventually be reduced to a bullet point or two on a resume. They can get what you offer – and much more – from countless others.

You don't want to hear this, I know. But your value proposition is commonplace, tired, and maybe even cliché to them.

The irony of this whole thing is that the Millennials probably don't even want to "Take Over." At least not in the traditional sense. They want meaning. They strive for some purpose in what they do. And they're looking for it in a place that looks and feels a heck of a lot more like a community than it does an institution. Could your workplace offer and even embody the things they are looking for? You bet. The good news is that Millennials aren't asking for anything that isn't already within our grasp… very much within our grasp.

Jamie Notter and Maddie Grant did a bunch of good old fashioned research from the trenches for this book. It's research with organizations that actually do this stuff with muscle memory. These are organizations who have Millennials, and Boomers, and X'ers like we all do. But these are organizations that have employees who literally say, "I can't imagine working anywhere else." Can you imagine? Kaboom!

I've been a Chief Human Resources Officer, so I'll be the first to admit workplace culture transformation is not easy, but it doesn't have to be complicated. As you go through *When Millennials Take Over*, you'll find a refreshingly actionable plan. One that succinctly lays out a blueprint for what the future of work holds. Why not spend some time thinking about how that future might be your present?

What we call the "future of work" today will very quickly become the workplace of the past.

We spend far too much time "catching up" in the world of work. We run at a feverish pace. But rarely is it a pace that moves us forward. We hire, for example, people that we need today; we don't attract the people who we'll need tomorrow…or a year from now. Organizations that figure out how to anticipate what's next, to listen closely to what their ideal workforce is drawn to, and then to evolve toward it with agility, are the only organizations that will remain truly competitive. In fact, they may be the only ones that will survive. Seriously.

You can practice this by listening to Jamie and Maddie and their Millennials. You can even just pick the one or two things that appeal most to you and start there. You don't have to become "the future of work" overnight. You only need to understand it, appreciate it, and then start moving toward it. The rest, I'm convinced, will take care of itself.

– Charlie Judy
Founding Partner, WorkXO (www.workxo.com)
June 2016
Chicago, Illinois

I firmly believe that progress changes consciousness, and when you change people's consciousness, then their awareness of what is possible changes as well—a virtuous circle. So it's important that the word gets out, that people realize what's working. That where there's been creative cooperation coupled with a communitarian view of our future, we're seeing real success.

- Bill Clinton, "The Case For Optimism," *TIME* Magazine

;)

1. Are You Ready?

What if you were responsible for hiring for a new position in your organization, and one of your young candidates showed up for her interview with her mom in tow? Seriously. She shows up for a job interview, accompanied by her mother. How would you react to that? This actually happened to one HR consultant who was hiring for a finance position. "I was shocked," he said. "How could she not know this was inappropriate?"[1]

But exactly how inappropriate is this behavior in this day and age? According to a 2012 survey of more than 500 college graduates, a full 8 percent of them were bringing a parent to a job interview. Google recently hosted a "bring your parents to work" day, in fact, and nearly 2,000 parents attended. LinkedIn (the company, as opposed to the professional networking site) held a similar event. What is so wrong about having parents included in the network of relevant work-related contacts in the business world?

So, which is it: an inappropriate gaffe from an inexperienced youth, or a harbinger of the new order in the business world?

Our guess is that the majority of the people reading this book will chalk up this story as an example of our inexperienced and perhaps even misguided youth. In fact, many of you may see this as yet another piece of evidence that this new "Millennial" generation (also known as Generation Y) is a real problem. Not only were they coddled so much as children that they need their parents with them on job interviews, they are showing up in the workplace expecting continuous positive feedback, immediate promotions, and unreasonable amounts of authority. But, before you stand up and shout "They just don't get it!" we'd like to remind you of a pertinent fact:

Every 20 years or so, a new generation enters the workforce, and the rest of us, quite frankly, freak out about it.

This is not new. Today, it is the Millennial generation (born 1982 to 2004) that is upsetting the apple cart, with what the older generations see as their sense of entitlement, informality, and impatience, but back in the 1990s, young Generation X was the "problem," with its disrespect for authority positions and overt cynicism. A few decades earlier, the Baby Boomers were entering young adulthood and throwing the older generations for a loop with their long hair, protests, and self-focus. Before that ... well, before that it was another generation with another set of faults. This has been going on since the dawn of time. As we will explain in the next chapter, historians have actually tracked the development of 18 distinct generations in this country, dating back to the 1600s. Each new generation brings a shift in values, so every 20 years or so we have to adjust to the newest generation that enters the fold. And, to be honest, all the teeth-gnashing and fist-shaking directed at whichever generation is coming onto the scene is mostly a waste of time. Over the long run, that younger generation always grows up to become part of the status quo. We have no idea if the Millennial trend to bring parents on job interviews is going to catch on or not, but we are crystal clear that the Millennials are not the huge problem they are often made out to be.

So, why do we focus on the Millennials in this book? The answer is deceptively simple: They happen to be at the right place at the right time. The Millennial generation is no better or worse than any other generation. That's not how generations work, actually. One is never really better than another; they are just different. But the Millennials are entering young adulthood at a unique point in our history, where society is poised for significant change, particularly around business, leadership, and management. In Chapter 2 we talk more about this historic opportunity, which we describe as a "perfect storm" of trends converging in a way that will generate an actual revolution in business. It is purely an accident of history, but the Millennial generation is entering adulthood and ascending into positions of power during this transition. It is not their choice, necessarily, but they will be leading this revolution.

We know "revolution" is a strong word, but when you look at the relatively short history of management, it becomes clear that we are on the edge of some rather profound change that is worthy of that word. The first revolution in management was its invention, approximately 100 years ago. In the late 19th and early 20th centuries, the building blocks of modern management were put in place as the industrial revolution was getting into full swing. We took a previously agricultural economy and transformed it into a juggernaut of productivity and efficiency using machines, chemicals, electricity, and this machine-inspired tool we called management, complete with organizational charts, job descriptions, strategic plans, and performance reviews. This first form of management revolutionized our economy and ushered in the modern era.

Since that time, however, management has not really changed much, even though our economy has been evolving at a rapid pace. We have gone through a depression, a manufacturing economy, a service economy, and an information economy. Today, of course, we are figuring out what the internet economy looks like, particularly after the "great recession" just a few years ago, yet throughout all of those decades of radical economic change, we have stuck with the same basic form of management that was invented 100 years ago. And frankly, it's showing signs of age, evidenced by how inflexible our organizations are and our consistently poor numbers around metrics like employee engagement. When you take this long view, you see that a revolution in management is not only possible but probably long overdue.

Capacities for the Future of Business

The decline of our century-old management model is just one "front" in the perfect storm that is forcing our hand in this management revolution. The second front is the social internet. While many people think of the social internet only in terms of transforming marketing, it has gone much further, facilitating a significant transfer of power away from central institutions and toward individuals. In our first book, *Humanize: How People-Centric Organizations Succeed in a Social World*, we explored in great detail the impact the social internet was having on leadership and management. We identified 12 different principles to help organizations become more compatible with today's social world: decentralization, systems thinking, ownership, transparency, truth, authenticity, inclusion, collaboration, relationship building, learning, experimentation, and personal development.[2]

But since publishing that book we have realized that **the social internet, despite its power, reach, and potential, was never going to revolutionize management on its own**. We needed another element, a catalyst that could connect the dots in a way that would bring a much needed management revolution to fruition. That catalyst is the third front in our perfect storm: the Millennial generation.

As the Millennials ascend into management positions over the next several years, they will simultaneously become the largest generation in the workforce. While the Millennials won't formally "take over" (no single generation ever runs things on its own), they will serve as a kind of secret decoder ring for all of us, helping clarify what the future of business will look like, post revolution. Their size, along with their generational alignment with the way the social internet has been changing things, will provide the ingredients that have been absent from our previous attempts to revolutionize management. We have wanted change for decades, but now, thanks to the social internet and Millennials, we are going to get it. The convergence of these trends is already in motion. Change is coming, and smart organizations will start making the necessary adjustments today to stay ahead.

We wrote this book as a guide for leaders who want to fully participate in this revolution, rather than be run over by it. What we in the business world need right now is a set of principles we can use to forge our own path in revolutionizing management. There isn't a set of simple answers out there that will tell us what the future of business will look like, but as we began our research for this book, we were confident that we could tease out the key principles to help us navigate these revolutionary times. Using our *Humanize* research on social business as a starting point, we chose two different research paths to round out the picture.

The first was to dig deeply into understanding companies with remarkably strong cultures. If traditional management is crumbling, we needed to better understand the "positive deviants" in the system—the organizations that were working remarkably well and attracting both engaged employees and more loyal customers. We didn't try to prove exactly what makes a strong culture (we don't think defining a generically strong culture is the point, actually), but, given that companies with average or ordinary cultures likely suffered from "average" (i.e., horrible) employee engagement, we knew we needed to draw from a different data set to extract insights that would break free from the clutches of traditional management and actually work in today's context. Through correspondence, interviews, and site visits, we investigated a dozen companies in a variety of industries that stood out based on their strong cultures.

Our second research path was to interview as many Millennials as we could in order to develop a more refined understanding of their approach to management. Again, we did not seek some sort of quantitative proof that the Millennial generation's beliefs about leadership and management as a whole are correct or the most effective. We looked for powerful insights. We looked for clues to help us make sense of this revolution that the Millennials seem destined to lead. We intentionally sought out the vanguard, the Millennials who were already inclined to be thinking about leadership and management issues, and then we asked them to reflect on what it is like to work in organizations today. We interviewed about 150 Millennial employees of companies of all sizes, for-profit and nonprofit, in many industry verticals. In fact, our research is ongoing, and if you were born between 1982 and 2004 and you'd like to share your thoughts on management and leadership in the workplace, you can fill in the survey (anonymously or not) here:

https://www.surveymonkey.com/s/millennial-research

We've sprinkled this book with quotes from this research, both positive and negative, about how Millennials see the business world around them. Look for them throughout and see if they reflect things you hear in your own workplace. We anonymized the responses in our research, and this is reflected in the quotes. You won't see any details about how big or small, for-profit or nonprofit the companies are that these Millennials work with—they come from all kinds of organizations. There may be someone quoted from your company. The point of these quotes is not to try to address the specific issues at these specific organizations but rather to draw out lessons we can apply to this revolution in the way we lead and manage organizations.

What emerged from our research were four organizational capacities that we think will prepare organizations to be successful, both today and into the future:

Digital
Clear
Fluid
Fast

The companies we found with ridiculously strong cultures had built these capacities into the heart of their operations and philosophies, and the

Millennials we spoke to could not understand why these capacities were not woven into every organization to begin with. Not everything about these ideas is particularly new—the push for more transparency inside organizations has been around for decades, for example—but there are unique applications of each of these capacities that specifically align with what is needed in today's context.

Digital

Digital is about perpetual and exponential improvement of all facets of organizational life using both the tools and the mindsets of the digital world. The industrial model of management was, quite simply, analog—mechanical and linear, like a pocket watch where you can see and control how everything works together. This allowed for organizational growth and improvement, but ultimately in a very limited and self-centered way. The organization became the center of the universe, and if our efforts to improve operations came at the expense of the customer or the employee, that was simply the price we paid for improved efficiency and productivity.

Digital in the Millennial era, on the other hand, has an unrelenting and disciplined focus on the customer or end user—including the employee. The social internet revolution showed us what this focus on the user looked like, when suddenly each and every one of us could become a creator and distributor of value, rather than only the institutions who had amassed the resources and infrastructure to do so. Millennials are the first generation to have only known a digital workplace, and they are used to being able to leverage that power on an individual basis. They are confused when digital tools are used for the wrong purposes or not abandoned when they no longer meet a need in the best way.

Digital organizations grow faster and accomplish more by focusing on the user, both internally and externally. Leveraging both the mindsets and the tools of the digital world, they break through the assumed constraints of the previous approach to managing organizations, unlocking new value continuously in areas like internal collaboration and even human resource management. We cover Digital in Chapter 3.

Clear

Clear is about an increased and more intelligent flow of information and knowledge that supports innovation and problem solving inside organizations. The industrial model of management linked information with power, so it tended to hoard information at the top, sharing it in a very careful and controlled way. We limited people to the information that they "needed to know." This approach, however, effectively lowered the quality of decisions in organizations, because what is "needed" varies by context and is nearly impossible to predict accurately ahead of time.

Clear in the Millennial era is about leveraging strategic transparency in systems to enable better decision making. The social internet was built on transparency, challenging traditional notions of privacy as we started sharing more and more online (particularly Millennials), and important phenomena like open-source software and Wikipedia were built on the notion of making what used to be done behind closed doors by experts now visible and public. Millennials have always had access to more information than they could possibly handle, and they are confused by organizations that control it tightly, since that approach just didn't produce results in their world.

Clear organizations make smarter decisions that generate better results. They need not be radically transparent (not all information will be shared with everyone), but they will successfully build a transparency architecture that makes more information visible to more people to enable better decisions. We cover Clear in Chapter 4.

Fluid

Fluid is about expanding and distributing power in a dynamic and flexible way. The industrial model of management viewed power from the perspective of control and thus as a limited resource. Power was given only to the parts of the system that were trusted to wield it, and sharing power (with other people, other departments, etc.) meant having less of it, so that rarely happened. As a result, power was mostly centralized, which unfortunately robbed organizations of agility. Again, today's complex and rapidly shifting landscape requires organizations to pivot and move in new directions more frequently, particularly on the "front lines" where value is created and exchanged. But, by the time the centers of power are able to make the decisions to change, those on the front lines who could act on it see their windows of opportunity close.

Fluid in the Millennial era is about systems that enable an integrated process of thinking, acting, and learning at all levels of the organization. The social internet revolution was based in this kind of action-learning. Power was decentralized, allowing for growth, change, and evolution that would not have been possible with a centralized approach. The Millennial generation, therefore, does not expect organizations to task the higher levels with the thinking and deciding and the lower levels with the implementation.

Fluid organizations serve customers more effectively and are more nimble in both strategy and execution. They may still have hierarchies, but they are created and maintained in a different way. We cover Fluid in Chapter 5.

Fast

Fast is about taking action at the precise moment when action is needed. The industrial model of management focused on speed in terms of efficiency and productivity. Fast was about getting more widgets off the line. As long as you could control all the variables, speed could be designed into the very details of your processes and systems. But, in a complex world, the speed disappeared. The complexity required new designs, and while everyone waited for systems and processes to be redesigned in our bureaucracies, opportunities were lost.

Fast in the Millennial era is about systems that can learn and adapt while still maintaining the efficiency and productivity of the previous era. The social internet facilitated this transition more than anything else. It transferred power from institutions to individuals, which gave more and more people the ability to take action, thus making that the standard. Large bureaucracies suddenly faced direct competition from internet-enabled startups, and the game changed. Beta testing became normal and expanded outside of the realm of software. We may call the Millennials "entitled" for wanting things right away or expecting more authority, but remember: That's all they've ever known.

Fast organizations leap ahead of the competition by releasing control in a way that does not increase risk. They go beyond efficiency and productivity to find the key variables that unlock true speed. We cover Fast in Chapter 6.

For each of these four capacities, we spell out in detail what they are, how they work, and what they look like. We tell as many stories as we can about the organizations that have already developed the capacities and integrated them into how they run their businesses. This is not speculative, theoretical content—this is happening in the world today.

We will tell you about a small nonprofit that has embraced the digital mindset fully, not only investing more in technology than some for-profit companies its size but also redesigning its workspace around the needs of the employees (and not just with a foosball table in the corner). We will tell you about a software company that is so fierce in its commitment to transparency that it allows its clients to come to the office and help with project planning. We will tell you about a healthcare company that frees up employees at all levels to make decisions and take actions when they have the right knowledge about the patient (including their hopes and dreams). And we will tell you about a bank that consistently outpaces its competition by investing in strong relationships, both internally and externally.

These companies are all tremendously successful by traditional measures, and their cultures are so strong that nearly all of the employees we spoke with could not even imagine working somewhere else. And they are doing all that by abandoning some of the core tenets of traditional management and embracing ideas that make a lot more sense to the Millennial mindset. These are the positive deviants. They are role models that are showing us that the management revolution is indeed possible. They make us optimistic.

We Are Optimistic

Optimism is actually an over-arching capacity that is critical for succeeding in any kind of revolution. Revolutions are never easy. If they were, we'd just call them change. That means you are destined to hit rough spots and setbacks that must be overcome for the revolution to succeed, and optimism becomes a critical element for success. If you lose your optimism, you stop doing the work. You stop maintaining things. You stop putting one foot in front of the other, and, when the moment for decisive action emerges, you miss the opportunity. Without a base of optimism, revolutions fail.

As we completed the research for this book, we regained our optimism. **We are ridiculously optimistic, in fact, about the future of business**. Not only were these positive deviants not that hard to find, they provided lessons that can be easily incorporated into most organizations today. In each of the chapters on the four capacities, we close with a section on how to build that capacity inside your organization. To be clear, we are not presenting the case studies in order to demonstrate "best practices." (If you read *Humanize*, you know that we literally think best practices are evil.) Your challenge is not to do exactly what these companies are doing. Your challenge is to learn from them, to use their experiences to spark a new approach to succeeding in your own context.

And yes, perhaps you can squeeze a little inspiration from these case studies, as well, and rekindle your own optimism. We will need some to make this revolution happen. Not coincidentally, optimism has long been identified as a key trait of the Millennial generation. When we first read that about Millennials, we were a bit skeptical, wondering if optimism might be more of a life-stage distinction than a generational one. Young people, in general, are more optimistic than the older population, regardless of the generational mix at the time. This makes sense: When more of your life is ahead of you, it is simply easier to think about all the possibilities. So, we thought optimism might eventually fade from the Millennials' list of characteristics. It is sort of like calling the Millennial generation "rebellious" because they are pushing against the status quo. That is not a Millennial quality—it is a youth quality. Every generation rebels when they are young, and we thought the same might be true about the Millennials' optimism.

11

But the oldest Millennials are into their 30s now. They have careers and kids and houses. Have they retained their optimism? According to one researcher, they most certainly have. Jeffrey Arnett is a developmental psychologist from Clark University and has been studying young people for some time. The university recently polled more than 1,000 people aged 25 to 39, which means half of the respondents were Millennials and half were from the younger part of Generation X, and the optimism was astounding. Arnett extended the age range in the poll specifically to see if tapping into the older cohort would reduce the optimism, but it did not. A surprising 77 percent of the respondents agreed with the statement, "At this time of my life, it still seems like anything is possible."

Arnett (who is not a Millennial) could almost not comprehend this level of optimism, as evidenced by his response in an interview with *The Washington Post* about that 77 percent figure:

> *That's less than the 18- to 29-year-olds, but it's still ridiculously high, like, what are they talking about? (laughing.) The vast majority (of young people surveyed) are in a relationship, have a kid, a job they've had for five years or more. How is anything still possible? I don't know. It's amazingly resilient, the optimism they've had since their emerging adulthood.*[3]

They maintained their optimism despite trying to get jobs during the great recession and despite carrying the burden of unprecedented student-loan debt. In other words, they are fighting the fight of the revolution, but they remain ridiculously optimistic.

We will explain more in the next chapter about the broader historical context of this management revolution, but we have seen a pattern of large societal changes happening every hundred years or so, and each time there is a generation heading into young-adulthood that holds us together with that surprising optimism and resilience. The Millennials are doing that today. The future of business is something that we all create together—every generation in the workforce. We all have a role, and part of the Millennials' role is clearly to bring that optimism. So, let's stop fretting about the Millennials and all their entitlement, trophies, and flip-flops, and let's focus instead on how they can help us to be more digital, clear, fluid, and fast so we can all get busy bringing to life a new era for leadership, management, and business.

The revolution is coming. Are you ready?

;)

2. Generations

If you are eager to dive into the four driving principles for success in our changing environment, please, go for it and head straight for Chapter 3. Digital, Clear, Fluid, and Fast are central to the future of business, and if we can get you to run with those ideas, then we will have done our job.

We do believe, however, that the most effective solutions in the future of business will be connected to today's unique historical context, so in this chapter we explore where all this change is coming from, and that means we should pause for just a moment and talk about everyone's favorite topic: generations.

We can guess what some of you are thinking:

Generations? Really? Haven't we heard enough of this generational hype? It's full of huge generalizations about millions of people that frequently don't match up with the actual behavior and attitudes of the people in my organization. And when we're not vilifying a particular generation as the cause of all our problems, we're putting it up on a pedestal as the shining example to follow. How does knowing about generations help me create a more powerful and effective organization?

We're sick of the hype, too. But that's part of the problem. **The hype and the oversimplifications that dominate the generations conversation have prevented us from seeing the serious implications that generational differences have for business.** Our research and experience says that generational knowledge is critical to succeeding in today's fast-paced, ever-changing environment, but the trick is figuring out which aspects of the generational field are relevant and which are not.

William Strauss and Neil Howe are arguably the most credible authorities on generations. This has been the primary focus of their academic career, and we consider them the go-to source on a topic that has no shortage of authors and consultants claiming expertise. Like everyone who writes about Generation Xers, Strauss and Howe have demonstrated deep knowledge about the differences among the generations in today's workforce—Baby Boomers, Generation Xers, and Millennials. What separates Strauss and Howe from their peers, and why we look to them as the basis for our thinking on this topic, is the depth and strong theoretical foundation of their work. They identify 18 distinct generations in the history of the United States, dating back to the Colonial era in the 1600s, and for each generation they make a clear and compelling connection between the generation's core values and the unique historical context in which it grew up.[4] As historians, they understand how the broader social and cultural trends shape and define the different generational cohorts, and their conclusions prove to be more useful and applicable than the other authors who pick random dates and use survey data to tell us how different generations think and act.

Furthermore, they explain how, once every four generations in this country, there is a major transition, which has a deep impact on our national culture, politics, and economy.[5] Interestingly, we don't tend to hear about this 80-to-100-year cycle in our history classes in school. Instead, we are presented with a simple, linear progression of history. We study the wars, the economic ups and downs, and the social and cultural developments, and it all seems to move forward along a straight line from the distant past on through to the present. But Strauss and Howe identify a deeper, cyclical pattern that more closely resembles the repetitive turning of the four seasons than a straight timeline from past to future. Each "season" in this cycle is represented by a single generation, which turns every 20 years or so, and every four "seasons" the cycle completes, marked by a major societal transition.

Strauss and Howe describe this pattern in great detail in their book, *The Fourth Turning*. When you look at the pattern, it's almost frightening in its accuracy. **Once every four generations (roughly 80 to 100 years), there has been a major war that marked the end of one era and the beginning of a new one**. The first transition was during the Revolutionary War in the 1770s, obviously a big shift as the Colonial era gave way to our first era as an independent nation. Flash forward 80 or 90 years from that point and you end up in the American Civil War, and then four generations later, like clockwork, there is another transition: the Great Depression and World War II, which represents the transition between the pre-modern and modern eras in the United States.

Here's where it starts to get even more interesting. **If you skip ahead 80 years from the Depression and World War II, you end up in the present, rather than the past. It's right now. Today.** 2010 to 2020. And, as the pattern would predict, four generations have turned since that time. The GI generation (also called the "Greatest Generation") was in young adulthood during the Depression and World War II, leading us into the modern era. Following the GIs were the Silent Generation, the Baby Boomers, and Generation Xers, and now we have the Millennial Generation entering young adulthood during the most recent "fourth turning"—a time that history predicts will be yet another significant transition, from one era to the next. So, are we really entering a fundamental shift between two eras right now?

Yes. And that is precisely what this book is about.

We cannot be sure of what the full extent of this societal transition will look like, but we are clear on one piece of the transition: business—the way we lead and manage organizations—is going to take on a radically new look over the next several years.

A Perfect Storm Transforming Management

Management is changing profoundly and permanently. That may sound like a dramatic statement, but there is more than enough evidence to support it. It's not that management is going away. We still need to scale effort inside our organizations, and that will continue to require the basic components of management: structures and processes that support collaboration, leadership—at all levels—that enables the right actions, and strong organizational cultures that make the whole greater than the sum of the parts. But the way that we do these things is now poised to change forever, due to three trends (let's call them fronts) that are coming together in a perfect storm, today.

The three trends are:

- The decline of traditional management
- The social internet revolution
- The Millennial generation entering the workforce.

Front #1: The Decline of Traditional Management

It may surprise you to learn that management was invented only 100 years ago. Certainly human history has gone through thousands of years of evolution in figuring out how to get people together in order to get things done (those Pyramids didn't exactly build themselves, you know), but management as we know it, complete with strategic planning, delegation of duties throughout a hierarchy, job descriptions, and human resource departments, is predominantly a product of the 20th century.

Prior to 1900 there just wasn't a need. The economy in the United States was mostly agricultural and entrepreneurial. The industrial revolution, which began in the early 1800s and started to pick up steam (pun intended) toward the end of the century, set the stage for modern management. But it wasn't until the early 20th century that the manufacturing economy reached the tipping point in its growth where the need for management became widespread.

And the brightest minds of the day responded. Frederick Winslow Taylor, now known as the father of modern management, was one of the first people to carefully study the process of working in industrial settings. Focusing on efficiency, he studied things like the perfect way to shovel coal and how to motivate laborers loading bars of iron onto railway cars. In 1911, he published *The Principles of Scientific Management*, and management was born. This code became the standard for the next 100 years. **Even today, we are still using the pay-for-performance principles that Taylor established at the turn of the 20th century, and many widely used management processes like strategic planning, performance management systems, and even some of the foundational concepts in the leadership field all have their roots in this approach.**

While one might have expected some change and innovation in this approach to management over the last century, its staying power is connected to its performance. The productivity and efficiency gains we have seen in our economy of the last 100 years are staggering. Industrial pioneer Henry Ford was able to apply the ideas in scientific management to his revolutionary assembly line process, reducing the time it took to manufacture a Model T from 12.5 hours to just 93 minutes. A decade later, Ford was producing nearly 10,000 cars a day, and nearly a century later, Ford was celebrating the production of its 350 millionth vehicle.

Our progress seems relentless and unstoppable, and fundamentally we have the revolution of scientific management to thank. Well, it wasn't only scientific management—machines played an important role as well. Our ability to master things like electricity, the internal combustion engine, chemicals, and telecommunication drove our productivity as much as management did. If anything, our machines inspired our management as much as that early research did. **Modern management treated the organization like a machine, with its component parts, flows of inputs and outputs and debits and credits, and an unquestionably hierarchical structure, where power and control were placed at the top or core because the periphery of the organization—the workers and employees—were expected to follow instructions and do their part, much like cogs in a machine.**

Over the years, researchers and practitioners have certainly launched some challenges to the mechanical approach to running organizations. As early as the late 1920s, researchers started examining the human factors in production, discovering that social factors influenced performance much more than previously realized, and things like group norms and the "informal organization" also played an important part.[6] In the 1940s, psychologist Kurt Lewin and others developed the new field of Organization Development, which focused on group dynamics and organizational learning. In 1960, MIT Business School professor Douglas McGregor published his management classic, *The Human Side of Enterprise*, which made the famous distinction between what he termed the "Theory X" and "Theory Y" approaches to management, with the X cohort of managers believing workers are fundamentally lazy and need to be coerced to produce, and the Y cohort believing employees are self-motivated and need to be supported to let their full potential be realized.[7]

These more human-centered ideas, however, have never successfully challenged the dominance of the machine model of management. Even though our economy and society have shifted out of the industrial and manufacturing age and into the information age, our mechanical approach to management hasn't changed. We have more laptops and cubicles than we do factory floors these days, but organizational structures, strategic planning, compensation strategies, middle management, and silo wars have remained. Our economy has changed, but our management not so much. Control is still the primary objective. Linear, cause-effect levers are the tools of choice for managers who needed to get the most out of their human "resources." And leadership is unquestionably tied to the positions of authority at the top of the organizational chart. We have been managing the information age using a machine approach.

But at what cost? **In the last decade there has been a growing body of evidence that suggests our machine approach to management may be showing signs of age, the most compelling of which is around employee engagement.** The most recent report from the Gallup Corporation on employee engagement in the United States shows only three out of 10 employees are actually engaged at work, and nearly two out of 10 are so disengaged that they are actively and intentionally making their workplaces worse. Just imagine the productivity gains we could have achieved over the last 100 years with higher engagement. A 50 percent engagement score still seems pretty embarrassing, yet it would represent a 67 percent increase over what we have now. And, as outrageous as these numbers sound, Gallup has been tracking these metrics since 2000, and they haven't changed significantly in more than 10 years. There are small variations year to year, but the basic ratio of about 30 percent truly engaged, 50 percent mostly punching the clock, and 20 percent actively disengaged has stayed the same.

We know that this is a problem, but we can't move the needle on a solution. The same can be said for the issue of organizational agility. Leaders from every industry complain to us about their inability to keep up with the pace of change, respond to customer demands, or adapt to the changing technology landscape, yet no one seems to be capable of coming up with answers to these challenges. **Not coincidentally, machines, by their design, are not very good at either engagement or agility.** Machines do not engage their parts in the co-creation of the work—they dictate the terms and demand compliance. Machines also do not change mid-stream. We have to take our machines offline and change them if we want them to behave differently. While our machine approach to management has taken us to great heights, the plateau we are on today is a reflection of an approach that has moved past its prime.

Front #2: The Social Internet Revolution

Against the backdrop of the decline of our traditional, machine-oriented approach to management, a separate storm has been brewing over a couple of decades that is going to actually increase the pressure on the old model. This second front in the perfect storm is the social internet, and

while most people recognize the significance of the internet in changing our society broadly speaking, not as many have connected those changes to an inevitable shift in how we run our organizations.

It is undeniable that the internet has changed our economy. Way back in 1999, *Time* magazine's prestigious "Person of the Year" award was given to Jeff Bezos, the founder of the online retailing pioneer, Amazon.com. Just seven years later, however, *Time's* Person of the Year was you. "Yes, you," the *Time* cover announced, "You control the information age. Welcome to your world." The award went not to a specific individual but to the millions of people around the world who were now creating and sharing content on the internet. In the first decade of this new millennium, the internet had been transformed into the "social internet." Blogs, YouTube, Wikipedia, Facebook, Twitter—suddenly the explosion of content, information, news, and entertainment on the internet was being created and shared in large part by an army of amateurs, rather than being in the exclusive domain of professional publishers.

As this social internet revolution spread, it became embedded inside our organizations, though not without some resistance. In the early days of social media, companies were caught off guard by social media, as evidenced by episodes like the "United Breaks Guitars" viral video or the mommy bloggers' backlash against Motrin, which implied in one of its ads that carrying babies in a sling might cause mothers pain. But, since that time, corporate social media has been catching up. Companies large and small are creating blogs, Facebook pages, Twitter accounts, and as soon as any new social platform becomes popular, the brands will soon be there. We are even seeing some companies becoming more strategic about their social media initiatives and raising the bar on ROI metrics. Marketing is flat-out different than it used to be. When Jamie recently tweeted "Is it wrong that I lust after a Chevy Camaro?" the GM twitter account responded directly to him within 15 minutes with a one-word response: "Nope."

Well played, General Motors, well played.

But here's the problem: Although we focus on marketing, the social internet revolution is actually much deeper. When you look past the new tools, you see a more important shift in society that has huge implications for leadership and management:

The social internet has permanently shifted the balance of power between individuals and institutions.

In his book *Igniting the Invisible Tribe,* Josh Allan Dykstra points out that before the social internet, four key resources in society were scarce and therefore very valuable:

- **Ideas**: access to the best knowledge, ideas, and information (through elite universities, libraries, or expensive encyclopedias);

- **Entertainment**: access to entertaining content (through television, radio, or the movie theaters);

- **Resources**: access to financial or physical resources (through banks and transportation networks);

- **People**: access to the people you need to help you accomplish things (through your personal network).[8]

Individual access to all those things was limited (hence the scarcity), and that made the institutions that controlled the access to these resources very powerful. Universities, banks, record labels, large corporations—we all needed these institutions to get what we needed. Today, however, that is not as much the case. Those institutions still have power, mind you, but our relationship to them as individuals has changed, because those resources are simply not as scarce as they used to be, thanks in large part to the social internet.

Now we can use Google to get access to information that used to be scarce. The elite business magazines like *Forbes* and *Harvard Business Review* are publishing large volumes of content for free, outside of their subscriber section. And even universities like Harvard, Stanford, and MIT are offering MOOCs (Massive Open Online Courses), through which people now have access to high quality education for free. YouTube offers more video entertainment than we ever could have imagined finding at a Blockbuster video store (remember those?), and as of 2012, Apple's iTunes store was offering more than 26 million songs for sale, which is quite a bit more than the record labels were sending to record stores when many of us were growing up. Even access to money is being disrupted, as startups can turn to crowdfunding sources like Kickstarter rather than being limited to traditional lending institutions. Where access to ideas, entertainment, resources, and people used to be limited, it is now abundant. In short, we as individuals have more power.

And we like it.

It's part of what it means to be human, actually. Psychologists refer to it as **agency**: that "subjective awareness that one is initiating, executing, and controlling one's own volitional actions in the world."[9] We are hard wired to want this, so the fact that the social internet has rearranged the game in our favor as humans is actually a big deal. It is no surprise, in that sense, that the internet played a significant role in the democratic movements of the Arab Spring that started in 2010. The social internet has no particular political affiliation, but it definitely likes giving power to the people.

Which brings us back to the crumbling machine model of management. Traditional management is dependent on the centralization of power and control, thus the social internet is only adding to the mounting pressure on the machine approach to leadership and management to change. **The more that individuals experience the new power that the social internet is delivering, the more confused and frustrated they become trying to operate in traditional bureaucracies and hierarchies.** And while the social internet by itself has not pushed traditional management to a tipping point, there is one more front in this perfect storm that just might do the trick.

Front #3: The Millennial Generation Entering the Workforce

We titled this book *When Millennials Take Over* for a reason. It's not that the Millennial generation is any better, smarter, more special, or more prescient than any of the other generations in today's workforce—it's not. It is simply because the Millennial generation happens to occupy a uniquely powerful position in our history. Millennials are the generation entering young adulthood as we undergo the "fourth turning" transition to which we referred earlier, and the forces shaping this generation are conveniently aligned with the other two trends in the storm that is forcing us to change the way we lead and manage. Add to this their size—the Millennial generation is the largest generation in the history of the United States, close to 80 million people—and the Millennials become a generation that will finally push the decline of the machine approach to management over the edge. **In 2020 Millennials will be the largest segment of the workforce, just as they are ascending into management positions.**

The perfect storm is here.

That means all of us (including those of us who are Millennials) need to understand what is shaping and guiding the Millennial generation. Unfortunately, this is where much of the literature on generations lets us down. Operating without a clear theoretical foundation, many authors end up contradicting each other and making claims that are difficult to justify, which ends up lowering the credibility of the entire topic. This is unfortunate, because the theory is both well grounded and easy to understand.

In short, **generations are formed by cycles in the evolution of our nation's history and culture.** Strauss and Howe identified the critical pattern that is at the foundation of the theory: Every 30 or 40 years there are trends and events that come together in a way that galvanizes us as a nation. Strauss and Howe call them "social moments" in our history, and the period spanning the Great Depression and World War II is a prime example of a social moment from the 20th century. The idealistic and socially revolutionary time that we call "the Sixties" in this country (which really extended into the early 1970s) is another social moment.

In each case, a generation of young people came of age (transitioned from childhood to adulthood) during those social moments and were thus significantly shaped by those historical events. For the Depression and World War II, it was the GI Generation (born between 1901 and 1924), and for the Sixties, it was the Baby Boomers (born between 1943 and 1960). Immediately following each social moment, there was a period of time when we recovered from either the external global crisis of World War II or the more internal social revolution of the Sixties. These recovery periods also each produced a distinct generation: the Silent Generation (born between 1925 and 1942) and Generation X (born between 1961 and 1981), respectively.

Every generation is shaped by what happens around them as they come of age:

- The Silent Generation, growing up as our country worked through and recovered from World War II and the Depression, has always been focused on security, delayed reward, and not bucking the system. They love command and control.

- The Baby Boomers, on the other hand, grew up during a period of social upheaval and revolution. They tend to value teamwork, group efforts, long hours, optimism, and making a difference.

- Generation Xers grew up as we recovered from the Sixties and were dealing with challenges like increasing divorce rates, corporate layoffs, and a surge in both parents working outside of the home. That's why Gen Xers are known to be independent, somewhat cynical, and adaptable.

This is obviously a cursory explanation of the characteristics of each generation in the workplace today, though it will suffice for the purposes of this book. If you're curious to learn more of the details, read Jamie's ebook *Generational Diversity in the Workplace*,[10] or you can go directly to the source—Strauss and Howe—and read either of their two books from the 1990s, *Generations* and *The Fourth Turning*.

Which brings us to the Millennials (born between 1982 and 2004). The Millennials are a bit harder to define, because the social moment that is shaping them as a generation is happening right now. It is harder to put your finger on a historical trend when you are in it. That being said, we're not going to sit around and wait 20 years to start understanding this generation, so we have identified four important trends that are happening right now that are shaping the Millennial generation as they come of age:

- The social internet
- Abundance
- Diversity
- The elevated status of children.

The social internet

The most obvious factor shaping Millennials (and one that pretty much every author on the topic agrees is important) is the social internet. The Millennials have grown up with the internet integrated into their lives. They take it as a given. They are not as amazed as the rest of us are at how fast Google can generate 5 million relevant web links in a matter of milliseconds (not to mention the fact that Google knows what you're typing before you've finished). That's not amazing—that's just normal to them. They've known no other way of retrieving information. And Millennials have specifically been raised on the social internet. They have been friending, following, and creating and sharing content since they were children. While we all have learned how to do those things in the last 10 years or so, the Millennials learned it when they knew no other way, and this has shaped them as a generation.

Steve Borsch wrote a brief paper on the "Rise of the Internet Culture" back in 2006. He interviewed some college students who were about 20 years old at the time (meaning they were born in or around 1986, which makes them among the early Millennials). These early adopters were already embracing a different approach to accessing content, using the then novel technology of RSS feeds, as Josiah, a 20-year-old college student reported:

27

I don't go actively finding information so much as I've used technologies like syndication and instant communication to set up a stream of information that comes to me, 24/7.[11]

Josiah went on to explain that when he found it difficult to find the information he needed, he simply found people who had the expertise and worked with them to create an application that would solve the problem. In other words, if they needed a problem solved, they took care of it themselves.

As Borsch concluded in his report:

This is not an unusual response for Josiah or many others: if something they need or want is not available, they simply figure out how to create it on their own. In fact, this behavior calls out a fundamental difference between those living in a participation culture vs. those who have come before.[12]

When you grow up in the age of social media and you buy a digital camera that doesn't perform in the exact way that you want it to, you simply reach out to your social networks and find out how to change it—or "hack" it—on your own. In the end, you'll own a camera that does things that the manufacturer may not have intended for it to do. This might sound disturbing to the manufacturer (and particularly its Baby Boomer and Generation X managers), but to the Millennials this is simply how you get things done.

This has some important implications for the workplace. As Millennials grow in numbers in the workforce, we will see more and more impatience with the slow speed of bureaucracy and the controls that limit action, particularly from people lower in the hierarchy. **The Millennials may not be the first generation to be frustrated with bureaucracy and hierarchy, but they are the first generation to have been given tools, on a huge scale, to get around them.**

Abundance

The second factor shaping the Millennial generation is abundance. There are more cars than there are licensed drivers in this country, and we actually spend more, as a nation, on trash bags than 90 other nations spend on *everything*.[13] Perhaps the most glaring evidence of the spike in abundance in which the Millennials are growing up, however, is self-storage. The self-storage industry rakes in $24 billion in revenue each year. That's up from $17 billion just 10 years ago,[14] and it has been the fastest growing segment of the commercial real estate business for the last 40 years.[15] There is now 7.3 square feet of self-storage space for every man, woman, and child in this country. Bear in mind, this is an industry that did not exist in the Great Depression. Back then, we did not have the "problem" of having so much stuff that we literally could not fit it into our houses, forcing us to create these auxiliary "stuff houses" to solve the problem (and, for the record, average home size was lower in those days, too). That's abundance.

When you combine material abundance with the information abundance that the internet has brought this generation, you end up with a generational cohort that simply has higher standards. They expect resources to be available, because they always have been. Basic needs are a foregone conclusion, so they look for more. If you want a cross-generational demonstration of the different experience Millennials have in today's world, just look at video games. Millennials are not the only generation to experience video games. Generation X grew up with Pong, Atari, and Space Invaders, but the games were two-dimensional and you could play with (at most) exactly one other player, who had to be sitting right next to you. In today's gaming environment, players can be immersed in a detail-rich, three-dimensional interface, with several (if not thousands) of other players online simultaneously. In the very popular game World of Warcraft, players come together in groups called Guilds, which allows them to leverage the different strengths of the various characters and be more successful in the game (the guild feature, by the way, was originally created by the users themselves, not the makers of the game). Millennials' gaming experiences growing up are abundantly rich, complex, and creative compared to those of Generation X.

Then Millennials show up in the workforce, where they are expected to follow orders, wait for others to make decisions, and do things the way they've always been done. This is a disconnect. Granted, every generation comes into the workforce and pushes against the status quo in some way, but growing up in the context of great abundance, Millennials are showing up with higher standards and greater expectations.

Diversity

The third social factor shaping the Millennial generation is diversity. This generation has grown up experiencing and expecting a greater amount of diversity in just about every aspect of their lives. Like abundance, this is not exactly a new trend, but it is rapidly accelerating. This country has struggled for centuries to embrace the inherent diversity in its population, particularly along skin-color, ethnic, and gender lines. Over the years we have made progress. Institutions and social contexts that used to be strictly homogenous—all white or all male, for example—have changed to become more diverse. One could argue it's taking longer than it should, but every generation of adults has been able to look back at the days of their youth and identify at least some increase in the diversity they came to experience as adults.

For Millennials, however, that trend seems to have been turbocharged. For example, consider the recent surge in the number of women members of the U.S. Congress. The first woman to be elected to Congress won her seat in 1916 (before women could even vote, actually), but even by the 1980s, women's share of congressional seats never reached higher than 2 or 3 percent of the total seats. As the Millennials began to grow up, however, those numbers grew rapidly. Between 1992 and 2012 (as the oldest Millennials grew from age 10 to age 30), women's representation in Congress more than tripled, from 6.2 percent to 19.1 percent.[16] By contrast, when Generation X was that age, the representation only doubled (3.0 percent to 6.2 percent), and when the oldest Baby Boomers went from age 10 to 30, the percentage of women barely moved, from 2.8 percent to 3.0 percent.

This is only one specific slice of the diversity pie, but it demonstrates a steep increase in the rate of change. **It's like we crossed a kind of tipping point, and now the changes related to diversity in this country are moving exponentially. Millennials now expect to be surrounded by difference.** Different musical tastes, different languages, different foods. Pen-pals from a neighboring state became replaced by large volumes of Facebook friends around the globe. Diversity has become an expected part of their lives.

An expression of diversity that Millennials are known to be particularly fond of is the "mashup." In music, artists have been using samples from other artists (typically from a different genre or era) for quite a long time. But with the social internet and the widespread access to music sampling tools, everyone started doing it. Even in the software industry, a mashup is accomplished by using code that was written for one application and adapting it for use in another one. Millennials are not surprised by mashups; they consider them normal.

So, now Millennials are showing up in the workforce not only handling diversity better but expecting it. **They are ready to color outside the lines, but more often than not they are met with the "we have always done it that way" syndrome.** This is going to be a challenge for a generation that learned to adapt to a diverse and changing environment.

The elevated status of children

The dramatic increase in the attention society paid to Millennials during their childhood is the fourth factor shaping this generation, and it is one that many people are quick to notice. As Neil Howe points out in his book *Millennials in the Workplace*, in the first year that Millennial babies were born (1982), we started seeing those yellow "baby on board" signs in the back windows of a brand new form of passenger vehicle: the minivan.[17] From the very beginning, Millennials grew up with the focus squarely on them. While Generation X children were dubbed "latch-key kids" because they had to let themselves into their own houses (empty of adults) after school, Millennials have been driven by one or both of their parents to soccer practices, birthday parties, and scheduled "play dates" with their peers from a very young age.

The constant presence of adults in the lives of the children ended up putting both groups more on the same level. In previous generations, when children and adults were together in the same space, the children were largely ignored while the adults discussed adult topics. Today, adults interact directly with Millennial children in mixed settings—in some cases on a first-name basis. And when the children do run off to play, the adults usually end up talking about topics like bad officiating at the soccer game or the dilemma about what kind of teacher gift to buy. Adult lives (of parents anyway) have become intertwined with the children's lives.

As a result, Millennials have blurred some of the traditional boundaries between themselves and authority figures. They are more likely to identify their parents as "friends" and "peers," and, as they enter the workforce, their behavior can sometimes confuse their Boomer and Xer managers who grew up with more rigid hierarchical lines. At a large healthcare company, one manager recounted the story of a young Millennial employee actually stopping one of the division vice presidents in the hallway to ask him a question. The older employees who witnessed the interaction were shocked and appalled. They knew that the proper protocol would be to email the VP's scheduler to get access, but such a slow and indirect route would never have occurred to the Millennial—and not just because of inexperience and not knowing the rules but because throughout his entire life he had likely never been denied that kind of access.

What Next?

So, what does this all mean? As we mention earlier, the Millennial generation happens to be the largest generation in the history of the United States, and they are now moving into positions of management. But we did not present the trends that are shaping this generation in order to convince you to be more like the Millennials. The Millennials are not the ones with the answers—no single generation is ever the one that gets things totally right. But at this moment in history, it is critical that we understand how the social internet, abundance, diversity, and the elevated status of children have shaped the Millennial worldview, because these things are shining a light on the future for us. The Millennials are serving as a kind of "secret decoder ring" for all of us, giving voice to the underlying trends that are pushing us toward a significant transition.

And the Millennials are just one "front" in this perfect storm. The decaying of our mechanically focused management should also be teaching us some lessons about what is to come, just as the social internet revolution should be providing some insights about leadership and management, not just marketing and communications. **The whole point of identifying the various forces that make up a perfect storm is to figure out how to navigate through the storm as safely as possible**. That is our challenge today, and that is the ultimate focus of this book.

In the next four chapters we will present four key capacities that organizations must develop in order to fully embrace this impending revolution in business: Digital, Clear, Fluid, and Fast. They emerged from our research and experience with cutting-edge organizations and with Millennials themselves, and we think they can help you make sense of the current trends. The decaying of our mechanically focused management philosophy, the revolutionary influence of the social internet, and the unique characteristics of the Millennial generation—now that you see how these big trends fit together, you can make the adjustments you need to steer your ship to safety—and further, to truly thrive in the future.

Let's get started.

;)

3. Digital

A few years ago, some Amazon.com customers complained directly to Amazon CEO Jeff Bezos about marketing emails they received that were promoting some, um, intimate products. It turns out that these customers had at one time visited the pages for some personal lubrication products being sold at Amazon. The Amazon system is constantly using algorithms to make recommendations to customers based on the pages they visit, and it pays particular attention to pages that were visited but did not generate a purchase. While customers generally appreciate these targeted recommendations, that did not seem to be the case when it came to these personal products. When the customers are unhappy, Bezos is unhappy (in case you were wondering, the arc between the A and the Z in the Amazon logo is a smile). The complaints prompted a tense meeting between Bezos and a number of senior executives at the company, including the vice president for worldwide marketing.[18]

Bezos' initial position in the meeting was to shut down 100 percent of Amazon's marketing emails until the problem was solved. This was a nuclear option, given that these algorithm-based marketing emails generated hundreds of millions of dollars in sales each year. But the revenue potential did not sway Bezos, who felt that **no amount of revenue could justify jeopardizing the customer's trust in the company**. In the end, as a compromise, they did shut down email marketing for some of Amazon's product segments, eventually instituting a system of filters that would stop certain categories of products from being promoted via email.

Meetings like this, called to solve problems based on the feedback of just a few customers, are not uncommon at Amazon. Many of the customer complaints that reach Bezos' email inbox end up getting forwarded to relevant staff with a single character added by Bezos: a question mark. Not all question-mark emails result in a meeting of the most senior leadership, but they all get some kind of response from staff internally.

It is an interesting paradox that a company as large as Amazon ($75 billion in annual revenue) will send staff off to solve problems based on the feedback of a few individual customers. After all, its growth has been fueled by much broader data analytics on customer behavior. Those algorithms that magically suggest the perfect additional product based on what you've added to your cart analyze huge volumes of data—not the anecdotal experiences of one or two customers. But at Amazon, it's a both-and, not an either-or. The big data analytics are critical, and the individual stories are critical. As Jeff Wilke, senior vice president for Amazon's North American retail operations opined in *BusinessWeek:*

> *Every anecdote from a customer matters. We research each of them because they tell us something about our processes. It's an audit that is done for us by our customers. We treat them as precious sources of information.*[19]

Customers are precious. They are unique and different from each other, and in the digital age it has become our responsibility to understand and meet their needs, despite the seemingly infinite variations. In the industrial era, Henry Ford could get away with declaring that customers could get their Model Ts in any color they wanted, as long as it was black. That doesn't fly in the digital age. Today we can email the CEO (yes, Jeff Bezos has a publicly available email address) and actually expect some action as a result.

What Is Digital?

We chose Digital as the first of the four capacities to explore because in many ways it may be the most obvious characteristic of the Millennial generation and the first thing Millennial employees will push to the forefront, notably through the use of social technologies. It is not surprising that Amazon.com is leading the way in today's digital age. Amazon was among the first of the online retailers to set up shop back in the 1990s. It not only survived the dot-com bubble; it grew to completely dominate the space and is now expanding into other ventures, including a multi-billion-dollar web services division and a company that seeks to reduce the cost of space travel. And it is only today, nearly 20 years into its existence, that it is even considering opening a retail store. Its existence to date has been purely digital.

Users First

But you don't have to be an online retailer or even a technology company to fully embrace what it means to be Digital. **Using digital technology is obviously a part of it, but it is really more about a digital mindset.** It is about organizing and working in ways that leverage and build off of what digital technology has made possible in today's world.

The Amazon story above illustrates one of the key components of the digital mindset: an unrelenting and disciplined focus on the customer. With computers and the web, Amazon can analyze customer behavior in ways we could only have dreamed of 50 years ago, allowing them to send customers—millions of them—customized messages based on their specific behaviors and tastes. Digital technology opened our eyes to the fact that customers are, in fact, "precious" resources, as the Amazon executive pointed out, not just faceless wallets that buy our products and services.

That kind of mindset can just as easily be applied without using digital technology. Happy State Bank is a large community bank in Texas that also has an unrelenting and disciplined focus on the customer, but its in-person interactions factor more prominently than technology. (You'll read a lot more about Happy State Bank in Chapter 6.) The culture at the bank is anchored around a deep care for customers, so if a customer calls in having difficulty logging into the online banking system, for instance, it is not unheard of for a bank employee to actually get in his or her car, drive 20 miles or more to the customer's home, and help the customer log in (and maybe get the internet router working as well). Whether using technology or personal contact, companies that embrace the digital mindset revolve around their customers.

Personal Service

The lesson here, however, is not just about excellent customer service. **The digital mindset is about enabling a personalized focus on the customer—on all customers—that was simply impossible in the previous era**. Before the digital age, companies could focus on a small number of customers, typically the ones that happened to be in the store at any given time, the ones that bought the most, or the ones who were most profitable over the long term. Because it was impossible to focus on all the customers, companies looked specifically at the most valuable ones. Think of a casino's attention to its "high rollers." Given the high volume of business these individuals bring to the casino, management gives them special attention. If a high-roller has a particularly unlucky night, the casino can offer some real-time customized responses, like "comped" room nights or free dinners.

In the digital age, that kind of attention is now available to a much larger group of customers, including at today's casinos. Caesar's Entertainment collects a vast amount of transactional data from all of its customers through its loyalty program, allowing it to give that same kind of high-roller service to a much larger number of customers. As Caesar's CEO Gary Loveman said:

> *You can't just fail to service the tens of millions of people that constitute the middle of the market.*[20]

In the digital age, the playing field in many different contexts has been dramatically leveled. This opens up new opportunities for more effective marketing, more effective customer service, and even more effective management internally.

Innovate or Die

Digital companies are constantly improving. In other words, they are committed to innovation. Innovation is a bit of a buzzword in the business world, but it is important that we define it clearly in this context. Some people think of innovation in terms of new product development, and others simply equate the word with change in general. It's more than that. We think innovation is focused on creating value, as expressed in the following definition:

Innovation is change that unlocks new value.

It's not just about creating value—it's about unlocking it. Innovation is a specific kind of change that recognizes there is value trapped in the old ways of doing things that cannot be released merely through incremental improvement. Innovation makes changes that are deep enough to actually unlock the new value. It is not just better reception on your flip-phone; it changes the game to create new value, like the iPhone did.

Innovation has been at the heart of both digital technology and the digital mindset. They're about continuous improvement and developing systems that can constantly make things better. Software is a product that is basically never finished. Each new release is designed to be better than the previous one. The digital mindset expects innovation.

39

[My company] has begun to "Red Tape"! This is a process in which teams have been created to focus on specific elements of technology in efforts to not only be up to date but be innovative in thinking and possible approaches. These teams are constructed of multiple individuals who touch multiple roles within the company. Red Taping allows for the select individuals to be the leaders in their area and relay the information back to the company via company meetings.

—*Millennial, b. 1984*

This is why we think of iconic technology companies like Apple or Google when we think of innovation. They are game changers, and they are not alone. Innovation and disruption (another buzzword, but one describing visible waves in the choppy seas of our perfect storm) have become a permanent aspect of the business world, particularly when digital and mobile technology are involved. Square is cracking the foundations of the credit card payment sector by enabling any individual with a smartphone and a bank account to accept credit card payments. Uber has disrupted the taxi and limousine industry with a ride-sharing smartphone app that allows individuals to earn money giving rides to others using their own car. Airbnb is shaking up the hotel industry by allowing individuals to rent out their own homes, apartments, or even spare bedrooms on a nightly basis. And instead of fighting this trend, some hotels may be jumping into this wave of innovation. Marriott now offers a Workspace on Demand program, through which you can rent out unused Marriott meeting rooms, using the technology of the office space innovator LiquidSpace (sort of like Airbnb, but for meeting rooms). **Companies that embrace the digital mindset can innovate business product offerings, innovate business models, and even innovate internal management processes with a sharp focus on continuous improvement.**

To recap, organizations that embrace the digital mindset:

- Put the customer or user first when it comes to decision making
- Provide customized attention to a much larger percentage of customers
- Commit to innovation and continuous improvement

They frequently leverage digital tools in order to fully embrace this mindset, though that is not the only path. Remember that the social internet revolution was fueled by a shift in the balance of power, away from organizations and toward individuals. That's why the digital mindset focuses on users and customers and expects things to grow and change constantly.

Why Millennials Care About Digital

And guess who else shares those expectations: Millennials. The Millennial generation is not going to wait for the rest of us to catch up with this digital revolution. As the first generation of "digital natives," they have a hard time understanding why the way things are done in organizations today seems to ignore today's digital reality. In a conversation about this, one Millennial asked a pertinent, rhetorical question, referring to the Boomer and Xer colleagues in his organization:

Why do they use email to send instant messages?

Millennials entering the workforce have already spent years using a variety of digital tools to communicate with friends and coworkers. As much as this draws criticism from older generations who fear that either their writing skills or their people skills have declined as a result, their digital skill base actually brings with it a more sophisticated understanding about which tools work for which purposes.

Let's say an older supervisor is heading to a meeting with a vendor about 15 minutes from now, and she realizes she needs some information from one of her Millennial direct reports, so she shoots off a quick email asking for the information. A few minutes later, when she hasn't received a response, she follows up with a phone call that starts with one of the most annoying sentences in the business world today: "Hey, did you get my email?"

For the Millennial employee (who hadn't yet seen the email), it is actually confusing that his supervisor would use email when she needed an immediate response. Why wouldn't she just use the instant messaging client? An instant message will pop up on the employee's screen (both his computer and his phone), so he will see it right away. Given the volume of email that he receives, he can't have every email notification on the screen, so the only way he would see the email right away is if he was checking his email every two minutes, which is incredibly inefficient.

> We don't use project management tools and don't invest in new technologies or upgrades to provide a great online experience for our customers. I feel like we are always a year or two behind—and it's always a clunky ride to get where we want to go. I don't know if our company is nervous about investing in a program (since there are so many out there), but something needs to change soon.
>
> —Millennial, b. 1989

Millennials are not just facile with digital tools; they understand that the tool itself and their own comfort with it are not as important as matching the right tool to the right job. When the volume of email makes constant checking inefficient, they move to a different tool that works better for instant communication. They are happy to use SharePoint for project management, but not if a group wiki would work better. They understand that solutions in the digital world are simply not permanent:

> *I think we've been adopting a mindset that nothing is ever "done." A website is never done, your email marketing program may become outdated, there may be a better LMS (Learning Management System) out there for us ... and so on. It's a little daunting, but I think the idea is to*

continually be educating yourself on new technology, having conversations internally about it, and networking with other professionals—because more often than not they're going through the same things.

Millennials are comfortable in a digital world where improvement is continuous and learning happens all the time. In fact, they are a little puzzled that their older colleagues do not have the same emphasis on learning and development:

I think that senior management is missing out on some great opportunities to learn and leverage some great tools. I certainly understand the demands on their time and sometimes other things take priority, but I would love to see more of a "love of learning" attitude among senior staff. As someone still fairly early in their career, one of my deep hopes and goals is that no matter where I find myself further along in my career that I will retain my deep love of learning.

When we asked Millennials the biggest single thing organizations needed to change in order to retain top talent, several pointed to better employee development. Millennials are typically characterized as being "entitled" in what they request for themselves so early in their careers, but it is less of a generational personality trait than it is their basic experience growing up in the digital age. The pressure to attract and retain talent is going to increase as Millennials become a larger percentage of the workforce, making the digital mindset inside your organization even more important.

What Digital Looks Like

The first place everyone looks when trying to identify a truly digital organization is on the technology side. Do employees always have the latest, cutting-edge technology? Has the company jumped into social media with both feet? Has it set up internal social networking capabilities through an online community, intranet, or instant messaging tool like Yammer? You get the feeling that, unless the organization is brimming with hipsters working at coffee shops on their MacBooks, iPads, and smartphones simultaneously, it can't be called "digital."

Not so. **Embracing digital technology is certainly a part of it, but it is really just a means to an end. The end, in this case, is the full adoption of the core principles of what being digital means: putting the customer or user first, serving the middle, not just the top, and continuous innovation and improvement.** You can use technology to achieve those results, but you don't have to. Menlo Innovations (discussed fully in Chapter 4) is a software company that definitely puts the user first, but some of its practices would be considered more "analog" than digital. Internally, the staff don't use email or instant messaging with each other. They all work together in one big room, so they use what they call "high speed voice technology" to communicate. When they need information, they just look each other in the eye and talk to each other. (Crazy, right?!) Their research on customer experience is not done primarily via the internet—instead they send staff they call "high-tech anthropologists" out into the customer's environment to experience that world first hand, in person. They embrace digital principles without over-relying on the technology.

Of course, if you want to use technology to embrace the digital principles of user focus, personalization, and innovation, that's fine too. TD Bank is known for its extensive and adept use of social media, even though it operates in the heavily regulated banking industry. Its use of social media internally helped it live the digital mindset by supporting innovation and continuous improvement. In one case, a junior teller expressed frustration internally about a paper-based process that she thought could be done better online, and when many other employees echoed that sentiment on the bank's internal networking site, the company took notice and changed the process. That's using digital technology (and the digital mindset) to enable innovation and continuous improvement.

> When you have, like us, a social collaboration platform where every project is just open and you can access all kinds of information, you don't need more. The only limit of that is, our search engine is not the best in the world ... ☺
>
> —*Millennial, b. 1987*

TD Bank also uses social media in its customer service, with dedicated staff to respond to customer issues on public social media sites. Those interactions are carefully monitored and archived to ensure they comply with regulations, but that doesn't stop them from meeting the customers where they are.[21] **These digital practices are rooted in a culture that has an explicit focus on putting the customer first.** According to Vinoo Vijay, the chief of marketing at TD:

> *The key to using [social media] well is really staying true to who you are as a company and what you stand for. ... And what we're about is service and convenience. As long as we deliver on that across all platforms including social, we know we'll continue to grow.*[22]

In other words, the tools are just tools. It's using the tools in a way that is consistent with your culture that really makes you a digital organization.

This connection with culture is critical. **Truly digital companies integrate the principles of being digital into the fabric of the organization.** So, that sharp focus on the customer or user actually translates to an equally sharp focus on the employee, not just the senior leaders in the organization. Providing more extensive service or attention to that broad middle segment of your market also means being able to address the needs of a much higher percentage of your employees, rather than just your stars. And commitment to innovation and improvement must be equally spread between your products and services and your internal processes and capacities.

Case Study: American Society for Surgery of the Hand

To show you what this looks like, we chose to profile an organization that does not match the stereotype for digital wizardry: a small nonprofit. The American Society for Surgery of the Hand (ASSH) is a nonprofit membership organization dedicated to advancing the science and practice of hand and upper extremity surgery. Founded after World War II by a small number of military surgeons, it now has over 3,500 members, and ASSH and the family of related organizations managed by staff bring in more than $13 million in revenue each year from a variety of sources including scientific meetings, journals, and online resources. It has only 22 full-time employees (FTEs), though, like all membership organizations, it also relies on a robust group of volunteer leaders to accomplish its mission.

They invest more in technology

Despite ASSH's small size, however, it invests relatively heavily in technology. Every employee has his or her choice of either an Apple or a PC laptop (which is replaced with a new one every two years), and on top of that they are each given either an iPad or Android tablet. ASSH's VOIP telephone system runs over the internet, and each employee has a headset, so phone calls can be taken at the employee's desk via the computer or basically anywhere via the laptop or tablet, including the roof deck (which does have wifi) or at home. Six of ASSH's 22 FTEs are working on IT or some kind of technology-related project full time. That's 27 percent of the staff (not including the percentage of time others might spend on technology-related duties), in a nonprofit sector that spends, on average, only 4.1 percent of its annual budget on technology (both hardware and software).[23] ASSH staff use internal instant messaging software. The ASSH website works on your mobile device. In short, ASSH gets digital.

One of the major projects at ASSH is a digital initiative called "Hand-e." (See it for yourself at www.assh.org/hand-e.) It is an e-learning portal where the organization is working to place every single bit of digital content ever created by the association and its members into one online portal. This isn't just archived newsletters. The portal contains thousands of hours of streaming video of actual hand surgeries, as well as conference presentations and online courses for surgeons. The content is available to ASSH members for free and can be purchased via an annual subscription for non-members. Members can submit videos as well. The idea is that hand surgery will get better when this content is in the hands (pun intended) of the people doing the work. The internet makes this possible, so ASSH has wasted no time in making it happen. There were already more than 500,000 unique pieces of content in the portal less than a year after it went live. In fact, the concept itself was conceived in a brainstorming session of members less than three years earlier.

They focus on internal culture

What makes ASSH a truly digital organization, though, is the way its internal culture embraces the ideas behind Digital just as much as its technology initiatives do. The digital mindset, as explained above, includes a disciplined focus on the end user and user experience, as well as enabling a larger percentage of users to get the customized and specialized treatment that was previously only available to elites. The Hand-e project reflects these mindsets as it makes a lifetime of content available to any hand surgeon who wants it, but these ideas are also woven into the culture inside the organization.

Internally, the "user" is the employee. A few years ago, ASSH bought a building and built out its office space and, being a digital organization, did so with a radical focus on the users—the employees.

Most office layouts provide offices with doors only to managers, with the larger offices going to the managers farther up in the chain of command. Those at the bottom of the pyramid work in cubicles. That's because most organizations don't think much about their internal users when they design their space. They think about the people at the top of the pyramid. At ASSH, the core workspace has all the employees in one large room together, with desks connected together in small pods. The CEO has the exact same desk setup as every other employee in the organization. (In case you think this could only fly in a small nonprofit, Zappos CEO Tony Hsieh has essentially the same setup, and Andy Grove of Intel was doing it back in the 1990s.) But it's not just the egalitarian nature of the setup that sets it apart. The entire office is designed so that every employee can find just the right space to get his or her work done. The desks themselves can be automatically raised and lowered to transition from a sitting desk to a standing desk. In one corner of the office, they have placed "tread-desks" that allow staff to walk and work on their laptops at the same time. There are many different quiet spaces to work in, ranging from traditional glass-walled conference rooms to a "yoga room," a coffee shop near the kitchen, and a roof deck that is outfitted with both electrical outlets and wifi. ASSH even has an "innovation ranch," which is a large room with spaces designed to spur creativity, including a loft that might be more accurately described as a bunk bed.

We know what you're thinking, but this isn't just an example of one of those "cool" office spaces with foosball tables and beer in the fridge we've seen emanating from the tech boom. **The space is truly, thoughtfully designed with the employee in mind.** Employees can choose where in the office they want to work, based on their needs. One staff person spends most of her time in the innovation ranch, while the finance director tries to spend a good part of the summer working from the roof. (Given that ASSH is in Chicago, that's probably about the most time up there he'll get.) And, of course, on top of this variety, employees are all given the opportunity to work some of the time from home. Two-thirds of the employees spend at least one day a week working remotely, but ASSH's investment in technology means that remote work does not interfere with getting things done or with being accessible to each other. When gasoline prices spiked, the organization expanded the policy to allow for more telecommuting days. One department has most of its meetings on the couches by the front door, even though they were not ostensibly designed for meetings. This is what a disciplined focus on the employee looks like. If it helps the employees get things done, then it is made available to them.

This is why ASSH invests in the right technology for its employees. It's expensive to make sure everyone has both the laptop and the tablet that he or she wants, but it enables employees to get more work done. ASSH recently decided to change its database system—typically one of the largest expenses a nonprofit association will ever incur—and the staff know this will disrupt many existing processes, but the old system was too slow and prevented employees from getting their work done. **Given the choice between hard on the organization and hard on the employee, ASSH will choose hard on the organization. That is the digital way.** Think software design: It may be difficult and time-intensive to design an app that works on iOS, Android, Windows, and (maybe) Blackberry—and the different versions of each—but that's what digital companies will do, as much as possible, because they know that a user-first, personalized approach is better in the long run.

And the benefits go to everyone, not just the elite in the organization. Entry-level employees are not stuck with five-year-old laptops with missing right arrow keys. Everyone gets new computers every two years. This mindset actually changes the way they do work. As one employee said:

This place cares more about us, so we should care more about this place.

ASSH has developed a culture where everyone helps everyone. Any time someone needs help on a project, people from every department are encouraged to pitch in. And if you need help on a project, there's no one you can't ask for help, and there is an expectation that you will always get help. Given that workflow can never be distributed evenly (for instance, the conference planners will always be busier right before the annual meeting), such a system helps ASSH efficiently manage the workload.

This structure also allows people to learn more on the job, working in areas outside of their regular job descriptions. **In fact, as a result, job descriptions frequently change from year to year as new strengths or passions emerge from this more flexible work arrangement**. This makes it harder on the organization. The CEO ends up doing employee evaluation and goal setting in different ways for different people and must adjust year to year as responsibilities change. But this allows him to maintain his focus on attracting and retaining great talent. He routinely is able to hire people from the corporate world into his small nonprofit, which is not typically the direction of the flow of talent in this industry.

We're working towards a culture of continual process improvement, which gives us ample opportunity to work on customer feedback and communication technology advances.

—Millennial, b. 1983.

They learn continuously and iterate rapidly

The continually adjusted job descriptions are also a reflection of ASSH's commitment to innovation and constant improvement, another core concept of the digital mindset. We've already talked about its commitment to changing or upgrading software whenever it's needed, and the Hand-e project represents a new and powerful idea that it brought to fruition very quickly. Mark Anderson, ASSH CEO, is addicted to change. According to one staff member:

> *Each year we have accomplished so much, and then we're going into something completely new.*

A few years ago ASSH focused on global expansion and quickly went from 100 international members to 600 international members in order to reach that market. It also made a rapid change to create an online version of a printed textbook in just six months. It did the same thing when it changed its annual scientific meeting to a paperless conference. Even back in 2008, when the economy started to take a nose-dive, Anderson pushed staff to identify efficiencies and new sources of revenue. When other nonprofit associations were using their reserves to operate at a loss during the downturn, ASSH was having some good years. According to one staff person:

> *We don't get too caught up in the major things that we're doing; we're always being proactive.*

Takeaways: Make Your Organization Digital

If a small nonprofit organization can become digital, so can you. Though, come to think of it, we can equally imagine large corporations complaining about their inability to be small and agile like the nonprofit. (The grass is always greener ...) But we did not present the ASSH example as a kind of "best practice" that everyone should copy. In every chapter, we will give you examples from real companies that are leading and managing in a way that is more compatible with today's reality, and we honestly don't consider a single one a best practice. They are meant to show you that any kind of company can embrace these mindsets (precisely because they are mindsets and not best practices), and to give you some ideas for how to do it in your own organization.

Being digital is not dependent on size or tax status. It is about an organizational culture (including systems and processes) that supports the digital mindset: a focus on users (and employees), extending elite treatment to the large middle, and continuous improvement and innovation.

> Many of our advances in technology where we can improve are surrounding productivity (internal) and digital presence (external), as business moves so quickly these days that it's difficult to keep up.
> —*Millennial, b.1987*

How small or large your organization is may change what that looks like, but it doesn't let you off the hook. So, here are some recommendations.

Invest Smartly in Tech

You probably saw this recommendation coming. Spending on technology, of course, is not a new idea. For years now, companies have been struggling with how much to invest in technology, which morphs and changes so fast that it is often difficult to figure out which investments will pay off. And since this budget item didn't even exist just a few decades ago, it always seems like it's a stretch when we do make an investment. No matter how much you spend on technology, it feels like it is just a bit too much. And now we're asking you to spend more?

Not necessarily. Start by taking a step back and comparing yourself to others in your industry. If you're one of those organizations that is down around the industry average for investment in technology, then you'll probably want to look for ways to increase that, but it's possible that you're already investing more than the average. In their book, *Leading Digital*, George Westerman, Didier Bonnet, and Andrew McAfee analyze a variety of different industries in terms of their level of "digital mastery," which includes a combination of digital capabilities and leadership capabilities. One of the key lessons from the book is that every industry has a continuum, from "beginners" to "digital masters." Even in the high-tech field, some companies were rated as "beginners," meaning they were behind their peers on both digital capacity and leadership capacity that supports digital innovation. And in fields that we don't associate with **digital mastery, like manufacturing, there were still a significant number of firms that the authors rated as digital masters. And according to their research, digital mastery correlates with both increased revenue and profit.**[24] It doesn't matter what industry you're in. Figure out how you compare to your peers, and unless you're already a digital master, find a way to increase your spending in order to increase your competitiveness.

Automate in favor of engagement

Notice, however, that we are not only asking you to invest more dollars—we are asking you to invest them smartly. If you decide to invest more in social media, for example, make sure your new program is not built around broadcasting cookie-cutter marketing messages to a larger number of customers and prospects through these new social "channels." That works, but it is not digital. **Digital requires a much more nuanced focus on customers: What is their experience, what do they need, and what matters to them?** Social media is perfect for discovering those things, but it requires that we listen and engage more deeply with customers and stakeholders. There are hundreds of books on social media marketing, so we won't go into detail on this topic here, but the most important advice we can give is to automate in favor of engagement. Figure out which things can be automated (feeds to social media sites), but not for "spraying and praying" equally to everywhere. Instead, use the time you save to spend more time building relationships with the people who respond, retweet, share, and like. When you invest in digital technology, make sure it actually addresses the core of what it means to be digital: It puts the user or customer first, it provides customized attention to more people, and it supports innovation or improvement.

Enhance digital collaboration

Not all digital investments are directed externally, either. Digital is equally applicable to internal capacity, specifically in the area of digital collaboration—using digital tools to help employees collaborate more effectively. As we mentioned at the start of this chapter, the Millennial generation is bringing with it some higher standards for technology tools we use internally and why we use them, so now is the time to up your game.

You can start with something as simple as email. For example, one organization we interviewed created a policy that prohibited sending "thank you" emails internally. It may seem insignificant, and maybe even a little rude, but this staff does a lot of work via email, so adding a layer of "thanks for that" emails, perhaps met with "no problem" email responses, can actually start to waste a lot of time. It's not that they are prohibited from saying thank you (they do that in person); they just don't misuse the technology of email to do it.

Apply that same kind of rigor to analyzing your other internal collaboration tools.

- Can you implement an instant messaging client to enable immediate requests to get through without the delay of email?
- Can you create an internal online community or other collaboration software that will allow employees across the enterprise to start connecting and solving problems on their own?

If you're not a leader when it comes to internal digital collaboration in today's economy, then you run the risk of falling even further behind.

Create Space for Experiments

Remember, your digital capacity is only partly about the technology. It is equally dependent on leadership capacities that support the development and implementation of the technology. So, if you want to be a "digital master," than you also need to make internal management changes that support the digital mindset. One of the most important areas to develop is the ability to experiment internally. After all, the digital revolution was brought about, in part, by the way it released products through "beta" testing, in which actual users could try the product and provide feedback before it was launched more broadly to the public. We need to infuse our organizations with the same capacity.

> I would allow for more calculated risks being taken. Everyone here is so worried about change. When you bring up a new idea it is usually shot down without any research or discussion.
>
> —*Millennial, b. 1985*

In *Humanize*,[25] we identified experimentation as a key element in creating a human organization, and in our discussion of experimentation we made reference to Google's now-famous (and recently modified—we'll get to that) "20 percent time" policy. Google engineers were able to spend 20 percent of their time working on any project they wanted, even if it was outside of their job description or outside of Google's core business. This freedom to experiment has produced some impressive results for the company. Gmail, for example, was created during someone's 20 percent time, and it had reportedly grown to more than 425 million users as of 2012.[26]

Of course, Google's commitment to experimentation is so deep that it had no problem modifying its own 20 percent time policy along the way. It was refined so only certain employees could use it, which was based on rigorous analysis of the company's own data, as is Google's way. So, Google doesn't have to be your role model here. It is not the only company that gives its employees room to experiment (nor did Google invent this idea). Forget about the details of Google's program, and build an internal experimentation system that works for you.

Give employees a sandbox

The real power here is in giving employees permission to experiment. Maybe 20 percent of your employees' time away from the core business seems too much. Fine. What percentage can you give them? Ten? Five? Maybe it's just a supportive place to talk about ideas that they came up with on their own time? Find a way to give your people some space. That is how you grow and improve: by shifting resources as things change. Yes, you might need to eliminate some activities currently done by staff to make room for the experimentation time, but find a percentage you can live with and give the employees permission.

Direct the rider

While you don't want to control the experimentation too much (that limits the learning), you will want to provide some overall direction, so the experiments end up supporting the growth of your business. The phrase "direct the rider" (alongside "motivate the elephant" and "shape the path") is the first step for change defined by Chip and Dan Heath in *Switch*, one of our favorite books about culture change, and that is your challenge here.[27] Define the goal of your X percent time program. It doesn't have to be only about innovation and new ideas. This space for experimentation could be used simply to spark engagement by giving employees more control over their work in general or a specific project. It could be set aside for cross-departmental collaboration. One organization we heard about involved everyone in helping to cut costs by giving them a target and letting them come up with how they were going to reach it. You'll have to figure out how this X percent time program fits into your success, and then you have to make that crystal clear to people.

Design a better feedback loop

And all of this experimentation is useless unless it can be fed back into the operations of the organization. These 20 percent time programs were never designed to enable free-range experimentation where employees ponder the origins of the universe. They are meant to be applied, which means that, as experiments generate results, the results need to be fed back into the system to see how they can improve productivity, inspire more creative product design, source better cost savings, nurture more engaged employees, or whatever the results might be. Your program needs a clear but simple process in place, so people know how frequently they need to report their results, to whom they will be reporting, and what criteria will be used to assess whether or not the experiments should continue. This isn't rocket science—actually, strike that; rocket science is all about experimentation—but you should be able to put a structure in place that will enable more experimentation in your organization.

Innovate Your HR Practice

If you really want to go "all in" on digital, you will have to look past the technology and even past your internal experimentation processes. The digital mindset is ultimately rooted in your culture. You have to be digital, through and through. **If being digital requires a sharper focus on users, internally that means a sharper focus on the "users" of your culture—i.e., your employees. In other words, if you want a digital organization, you need a culture that is employee focused.** That puts the Human Resources function in the spotlight, which for many organizations can be a real problem, because the HR function tends to reflect the old, mechanical approach to management. It focuses primarily on the organization and its leaders—not the employees. You may not think about this kind of change first in your move to be digital, since it is not about technology, but to be truly digital you need to do HR differently.

Hire for culture fit and personal growth

Job descriptions, for example, are created with the organization's needs in mind. They are designed in the abstract, and then HR's job is to find candidates that match those generic descriptions. There's no rule saying it has to be that way. At ASSH, for example, job descriptions are modified each year based on how each individual employee is developing. When they hire people, they put them through a day's worth of personality tests to determine if the candidates will be a good fit for their culture and will thrive in an environment where standards are high, collaboration across department lines is expected, and technological proficiency is valued. If you're going to really focus on the employees, then you need to take the time and effort to actually get to know them. At ASSH, that means they sometimes turn down someone with a master's degree (which might fit the job description better) and hire someone right out of school, but the culture is stronger for it and they can maintain their disciplined focus on the employees.

More and more organizations are abandoning what have traditionally been deemed "best practices" in the HR world. Menlo Innovations (featured in Chapter 4) specifically hires for what it calls "kindergarten skills," knowing it can train for technical skills later. Buffer, another technology company, also eliminated the technical interview in its hiring process, focusing only on culture.[28] Both companies then hire people on a short-term basis at first so they can actually see candidates' technical work in the real world. Truly embracing the digital mindset requires a sharper focus on your employees, so change your hiring processes so they actually do focus on employees.

Fix your performance review process

The performance review is another HR process that is stuck in the old model, thus it is ripe for change. The annual review process in which a single score determines a bonus actually causes a lot of unnecessary stress for the employee. Australian software company Atlassian has reversed the process and focuses more on ongoing coaching for employees.[29] Healthcare company QLI (which you'll read about in Chapter 5) lets employees develop their own leadership development plan. Then the plan is shared with the specific individuals who will be able to give the most effective feedback in the areas of development identified, even if those people are on different teams or different levels in the organization. At Menlo Innovations, reviews are done at the employee's discretion, involving whomever the employee chooses to participate in the peer feedback session. It is made clear to those who want to advance in the organization that they should include some of their harshest critics in the feedback sessions—and Menlo makes sure they hire people who have a natural ability to handle both giving and receiving constructive criticism.

Some companies are going so far as to rethink the entire employee/employer relationship. In their book, *The Alliance*, Reid Hoffman (cofounder of LinkedIn), Ben Casnocha, and Chris Yeh present a model of employment where the organization and the employee negotiate a series of "tours of duty." For each tour, the employee and the company clarify what each side gets out of the relationship, offering a number of different types of tours to guide employees at different stages of their career. This perfectly reflects the digital mindset's emphasis on offering more to what they call the "middle class" of employees:

> *Companies have long devoted resources to crafting personalized roles and career paths for their stars. Companies such as General Electric rotate promising young executives through a series of assignments to help them gain experience in different functions and markets. Yet it is possible—indeed, necessary—to extend this personalized approach to all employees using the tour of duty framework. As the world becomes less stable, you can't just rely on a few stars at the top to provide the necessary adaptability.*[30]

The human resources department is fertile ground for reinvention based on a digital mindset. Schedule time with your HR department to break down your basic HR processes in terms of how they address the principles that drive Digital:

- What can you add to your standard hiring process that would enable you to better understand your candidates as whole people?

- Do your performance reviews give space for each individual employee to understand and articulate his or her life's direction, so those goals can be woven into performance and learning objectives?

- How are you integrating short-term assignments into the hiring process, in order to get more reliable data around both technical and collaborative skills?

From Digital to Clear

We identified three relatively obvious areas that are ripe for improvement in most organizations: technology investment, experimentation, and HR practices. Obvious, though, does not mean easy to do. Approaching these through the digital mindset is the key to making them happen, regardless of budget concerns or embedded aversion to change. The digital mindset is about a relentless focus on the user (both external with customers and internal with employees), the ability to personalize their experiences, and continuous innovation—unlocking new value through learning and improvement. Why the digital mindset? Because the Millennial generation has grown up with this mindset like breathing air. It's not the pot of gold at the end of the rainbow for them; it's the basic way things work in the world outside of the office, and it will be the first thing they change inside the office when they become senior enough to do it. Remember, the Millennials are not telling us how to do things, but they are shining a light on the capacities that will drive this revolution in leadership and management.

So, if Digital is the bottom rung of the ladder, what's the next step? Let's talk Clear.

;)

4. Clear

General Stanley McChrystal led the Joint Special Operations Command for the U.S. Military for five years, between 2003 and 2008. Much of that time was spent leading operations against Al Qaeda in Iraq, immediately following the fall of Baghdad. This was no easy task, of course, but to make matters worse McChrystal discovered early on that the way his forces were trained and organized to do their jobs was actually making the job more difficult.

McChrystal's forces needed to dismantle an enemy network, which was less about the iconic image of columns of tanks rolling across the battlefield and more about smaller, focused operations—an iterative process of gathering intelligence, analyzing it, and using the insight to direct the next intelligence-gathering mission. The problem, however, was that this basic process was being managed by several different intelligence-gathering agencies and units under his command at the same time, and they were not inclined to share information with each other. When he first started, it took weeks to get the analyzed intelligence back from one operation. In August 2004, his task force was completing 18 operations per month, which was considered to be a high-speed operation at that time, but, in McChrystal's own words, those efforts "couldn't make a dent in the exploding insurgency."[31]

Two years later, the task force was completing 300 operations per month. He had created his own network to fight Al Qaeda's, and it was operating at a speed that he admitted was not even considered before, not in their "wildest dreams." This new network produced results. In 2006, McChrystal's forces took down the leader of Al Qaeda in Iraq.

Achieving this kind of success is impressive in its own right, of course, but it is even more impressive when you consider the level of internal change that was required to see it through. McChrystal and his colleagues had to fundamentally change the culture of this particular part of the U.S. military to achieve these goals. His realm covered special forces, the intelligence community, and covert operations, yet he succeeded by embracing a principle you might not expect from this group:

Transparency.

McChrystal learned that, in a war of networks versus networks, you need power spread among the periphery, because that's where the action is. "You can't centralize 10 raids a night," he explained. In this context, that meant sharing more information internally, so you don't have to wait weeks to get your intelligence analysis back. The military (and plenty of other organizations) have traditionally adopted a "need to know" policy on information sharing: Unless you can demonstrate a clear need to know, we're not going to tell you. In Iraq, however, McChrystal came to the realization that the challenge was not about demonstrating a need to know; the challenge was understanding who actually needed to know what information in the first place.

In a complex, connected, and networked environment, it is extremely difficult to know who needs to know. You just can't predict that ahead of time. The answer to this conundrum was to share the information more broadly. The more people who know, the more likely the person who actually does need it will end up getting it. At one point during his command, his group acquired personnel records from the enemy. To enable his network to take action on this information right away, he declassified the intelligence. He said he took a lot of flack for that decision, but making the information more visible enabled the right people to make better decisions and take more effective action. From McChrystal's 2010 TED talk:

> [A]s we passed that information around, suddenly you find that information is only of value if you give it to people who have the ability to do something with it. The fact that I know something has zero value, if I'm not the person who can actually make something better because of it. So, as a consequence, what we did was we changed the idea of information, instead of knowledge is power to one where sharing is power. It was the fundamental shift, not new tactics, not new weapons, not new anything else. It was the idea that we were now part of a team in which information became the essential link between us, not a block between us.[32]

In the last chapter, we discussed the idea of the digital mindset being the "ground floor" of what it means to be a 21st-century company. If you take that to heart, and your company focuses on the users, personalizes their experiences both inside and out, and commits to innovation, then how do you keep everything focused? How do you keep your collective eyes on the prize? By being **Clear**.

What Is Clear?

We started this chapter with McChrystal's story for two reasons. First, it was one of the best illustrations of the value of clarity inside an organization that we could find. The clarity existed at multiple levels. Not only did he declassify intelligence to ensure it was widely shared; he also had his officers work together in "situation rooms" rather than in single offices (yes, even in tents in the desert, office space design matters) to make sure everyone was on the same page. They were clear on their purpose, and they were even clear on why clarity was so important: because only a network can defeat a network.

The second reason we started with this story was to make a preemptive strike against your excuses. This is the Joint Special Operations Command for the U.S. Military, an organization with "secrecy in its DNA," according to McChrystal. If a secretive group like this can embrace clarity, then how could you possibly argue that it won't work for your organization?

Well, quite easily, it turns out, at least historically speaking.

The Myth of Control

One of the most central tenets of management over the past 100 years has been the control of information. From a competitive point of view, many types of information—secret formulas, strategic initiatives, and the like—should be controlled to prevent your competitors from gaining an advantage. Too much information in the hands of the "wrong" people is dangerous to the health of the enterprise. Knowing this, we have learned to carefully craft our messages and massage our numbers before they are released, all in order to protect our interests and mitigate risks.

Inside the organization, too, information has traditionally been tightly controlled. It's not that we, as leaders, fear our own employees will use information against the interests of the company. It's more basic than that: We are afraid of incompetence.

> I won a spot bonus but had no idea what the process was that determined who received spot bonuses and was looked at like I was crazy when I asked about it. I know when I first started, even the onboarding process had an esoteric feeling to it, where it was like unless you knew people with information a lot of things you would never find out.
>
> —Millennial, b. 1988

There is an underlying assumption in management that releasing too much information will lead to chaos, mistakes, misinterpretations, inefficiency, and an overall lack of coordinated effort, simply because humans are not perfect. It's like the childhood game of "operator," where a short phrase, when whispered from one person to the next around the circle, emerges as a completely different phrase when it comes back around. Given the complexity and scope of our organizations, such a tendency can be dangerous. The more information that is out there, the more mistakes will be made. The solution we devised to this problem is to give the people at the top of the system control of the information and decide what is shared, how it is shared, and with whom it is shared. Controlling information gives you efficiency and productivity, even if it means a direct relationship between your position in the hierarchy and the amount you know about what's really going on.

Controlling information inside organizations applies horizontally as well as vertically. Different departments, teams, and units are stingy when it comes to sharing information outside of their domain. Sometimes it's rooted in internal competition for resources, but more often it is simply a lack of trust in the competence of others. It's easier to keep all your information within your team so you can get the job done. It wastes time to explain things to people in other departments, and they lack the specialized knowledge you have in your department, so they will probably screw it up. By hoarding information, according to traditional management practices, we end up reducing mistakes.

While the logic of controlling information is compelling (efficiency, productivity, fewer mistakes), it is unfortunately disconnected from today's reality. This is essentially what McChrystal realized in Iraq. Using traditional methods to deal with today's networked, distributed enemy wasn't going to work. Today's leaders in organizations are faced with the same kind of challenge. Controlling information ends up creating more problems than it solves. More specifically, **the opportunity costs of not liberating information are staggering compared to the benefits of controlling it**.

When you share more information, you end up putting it in the hands of people who can use it, which expands the capabilities of the whole system.

This has been one of the fundamental lessons of the social internet. Take open-source software, for example. By sharing the code and letting everyone change it, something interesting happened. Instead of resulting in some kind of chaotic mess that traditional management might predict would happen when letting go of control, the software actually became more stable. Making it open allowed the right information to make its way into the right hands: specifically, people who were so passionate about the software in question that they would work on it for free. Trying to find those people ahead of time in a planned and controlled way would have been difficult, if not impossible, but by making the software open and accessible they built the capacity of the system to be more effective, without trying to control it. By seeing more, the individual coders ended up making smarter decisions along the way, and the entire product was greatly improved.

> [If I were in charge,] I would create an environment free from silos. All departments would fully understand how work in one area of the business affects another. I would also encourage employees to work wherever they are most productive. I think the traditional office setting is quickly changing.
>
> —*Millennial, b. 1986*

Sharing by Default

That is the essence of Clear: making more information available to more parts of the system to enable better and more strategic decision making, thus improving results. The default is that information is shared, not private. While this concept is not new (open-book management has been around for 20 years, with the same basic objective in mind), what we are seeing today is a seismic shift, where transparency and information flow are being transformed from a couple of occasional, nice-to-have features into the very foundation of an enterprise's power and agility. **Clear organizations start with the assumption that information is and should be available, and then they sharpen the focus to ensure that precisely the right information ends up in precisely the right place, relying on the power of an intelligent,**

decentralized system rather than central control. The result is more effective decisions throughout the system. Clear organizations make consistently smarter decisions, even in a complex and rapidly changing environment.

Why Millennials Care About Clear

Millennials, of course, would have it no other way. While the rest of us are trying to deal with today's world of "information overload," to Millennials, it's just normal. They have always had Google. They don't know what it's like to *not* have a staggering amount of information, available within milliseconds, and delivered to a powerful computer that you keep in your pocket and works wherever you are. Back to the Roots (a hydroponics company we will talk more about in Chapter 6), where all 15 staff are Millennials, has a saying that "I don't know" is never an acceptable answer. For this generation, "I don't know" means you haven't looked on the internet yet, you haven't tapped into your social networks yet, and you haven't leveraged technology or software to experiment your way to an answer. This generation does not pretend to have all the answers (any more or less than any previous generation has at that age), but Millennials do assume they will have access to whatever information they need, because it has always been there.

When Millennials show up in the workforce, many of them scratch their heads about why organizations seem to be stingy with information, particularly up and down the hierarchy. In our research, we asked Millennials in the workplace about how their organizations deal with an increased demand for transparency, and, more often than not, they expressed frustration. One Millennial working at a publicly traded company reported:

> *We are subject to public disclosure but still do not have transparency internally. Decisions are made behind closed doors, and the reasons behind the decisions are not often cited when handed down.*

Others we talked to complained of being held accountable to implement decisions that were made at meetings that they did not even know about, let alone understand what was decided at those meetings.

There is little to no transparency at my company. Lots of closed-door meetings with no follow-up as to what the meetings revolved around. There have been times where there have been exclusive meetings and then there is an expectation for the younger workforce to complete the work that was discussed in that exclusive meeting.

To some extent, every generation enters the workforce with some frustration about not being in the know—that is the nature of our hierarchical management model, so that was also the experience of Generation Xers, Baby Boomers, and even the Silent Generation as they entered the workforce. The young people at the bottom of the pyramid are usually frustrated. But today's frustration seems a bit more sophisticated. **It's not just the frustration of having very little power—we've all felt that. It's frustration that the organization is missing opportunities**. Listen to this Millennial employee:

Our organization has quarterly office meetings where they talk about financials and benefits and profit sharing and whatnot, but other than that there isn't much transparency. The workers are kept in the dark about what is said about the company externally and how they get clients in. We don't know if they are over-promising our capabilities and capacity for work. I don't think my company even realizes that transparency is even changing.

That's a 25-year-old who is concerned about the organization's capacity to get work done and bring in the right clients. Not exactly the entitled, impatient, all-about-me Millennial who you were expecting, is it? That's a young person who grew up understanding that access to information is directly correlated with ability to take action. It may have started out as something fairly insignificant, like using social media to find the coffee shop or happy hour where they could meet people who they enjoyed spending time with, but the principle has stuck with them. They understand the value and the inherent potential of transparency, and they are perplexed at the leaders of today's organizations who seem to be missing this opportunity.

> Our shared common drive has access to all work-related files. Anyone within the company can access the board of directors report, our internal audit, or practices manual (to name a few) and have the same information as our leadership team. When questions are asked, the organization seeks to provide information in a way that actually explains changes or thinking behind a decision versus simply "because it has to happen."
>
> —*Millennial, b. 1986*

What Clear Looks Like

For those of you who don't want to miss this opportunity, you need to understand what clear actually looks like. As you might have guessed, there is no one, right way to make your organization clear; it is not some kind of binary choice, where you are clear or not clear. It is a blend. All organizations will strike a balance between what is shared and what is kept private, and the mix will vary depending on the context. So, leveraging the power of transparency requires a sophisticated application of the concept. You don't just share information to be clear. You need to share it strategically.

For example, in *Humanize*,[33] we told the story of how Whole Foods, Inc. actually shares all of its salary and bonus data internally. In other words, everyone at Whole Foods knows how much money everyone else makes (or at least they have access to that information if they want it). Judging from the reactions we get from conference audiences when we tell this story, this is not a common practice. In fact, the idea seems to scare people.

But Whole Foods doesn't share this information just to be provocative. It shares compensation info (and other business data as well) to enable the individuals and teams at their stores throughout the country to make better decisions. Bonuses at Whole Foods are team based, so if you manage the produce department at a Whole Foods in Orlando and your department achieves certain metrics, it triggers a bonus for your whole team. By making

salary and bonus data available, you could see, for example, when the produce team in Nashville suddenly starts making big bonuses, and you could
reach out to them to see what they are doing to achieve those results. You
could then learn from their experience and apply that insight to your own
store. And if it works, of course, your team will then get bonuses, and you
may find the produce manager from Sacramento calling you to learn from
your experiences.

**The end result is a system that is agile and can make quick changes
based on market conditions, without the center of the organization having to figure it all out and tell the stores what to do.** The system learns from
itself, makes better decisions, and performs better, but that layer of transparency enables these results. That is an example of being strategic when
introducing clarity into your organization.

Again, sharing financial data is probably the most common form of
clarity organizations are introducing, even though most fall short of reveal-
ing salary and bonus information. Open-book management is designed to
educate all employees about the basic financial and operational health of the
organization so that, armed with that knowledge, each employee will make
better decisions to support the financial growth of the company. The idea
can be applied in many different contexts. Morning Star, a large tomato
processing company, has enabled every team to understand its own profitability, and so it allows every single employee to buy whatever equipment he
or she needs to get the job done. On the other end of the spectrum, a small
clam shack in Maine educated all of its staff about financial and operational
details and immediately saw bottom-line results as the staff started making
improvements on their own, down to the frequency of cooking-oil changes
and the placement of pencils for customer comment cards.

[If I were in charge, I would have] more honesty and transparency from
management. Equality among all employees. All staff would be considered a "family" unit, regardless of their income or family status.
—*Millennial, b. 1984*

But, to do clarity right, it must go beyond the financial and business model implications. The effectiveness of decisions is not always tied directly to financial outcomes, so if that is the only kind of information you are willing to liberate, you will limit the effectiveness of your clarity efforts. Consider the case of the software company Menlo Innovations.

Case Study: Menlo Innovations

Menlo Innovations designs and builds custom software at its headquarters in Ann Arbor, Michigan. About 50 people work in its large, one-room, open-space office, developing software for a variety of clients, including biotechnology companies, universities, nationwide foodservice organizations, and large healthcare companies. Menlo's mission as an organization is "to end human suffering in the world as it relates to technology."[34] Software, but without suffering? That must be some pretty good software. And, judging by Menlo's consistent growth over the years, as well as the impressive demand to work there (when a position opens up at Menlo, it gets enough applicants to bring in 30 people at a time for an initial group interview), it seems to be hitting the mark.

As a company, Menlo Innovations has achieved some notoriety in the business press for its innovative approach to management. CEO Rich Sheridan has written an excellent book about his journey in creating and growing Menlo (see *Joy, Inc.*), and articles in *Forbes* and on NPR have highlighted some of the interesting features of its workplace, like the lack of offices (everyone works on moveable tables spread throughout one big room) and how the programmers work in pairs (literally one computer shared by two programmers), switching pairs every week.

They work out loud

What interested us, however, was the way Menlo embedded clarity so deeply inside the organization. Take its practice of pair programming, for example. The practice was not invented at Menlo; it is an aspect of Extreme Programming, a practice developed in the 1990s (and one that inspired Menlo CEO Rich Sheridan to create his company the way he has). Pair programming is clarity in action. Typically, software is reviewed and tested after it is created; that's where you find and fix the bugs. In pair programming, however, one of the programmers is always reviewing the code, as it is *being written*, which has been shown to increase the quality of the code.[35] In traditional companies, lone programmers write their code in private, essentially, but at Menlo **the process of coding is made more transparent, which improves the decision making of both programmers who are working in the pair.**

They make their culture visible

And that's just the beginning of transparency at Menlo. Its project management system also promotes clarity. It is perhaps ironic, given that the employees write software for a living, that Menlo does not use a computer-based project management system. Its system is literally attached to the walls of the office and consists primarily of handwritten note cards, colored stickers, and yarn. Each project identifies specific tasks that are written on the cards and assigned to programmer pairs at the beginning of a week and placed on the wall based on the day they think they will get to that task. There are five rows on the wall, corresponding to each day of the work week. They use colored stickers to indicate progress on the tasks, and they simply move a line of yarn down at the end of each day as the week progresses.

Any staff person can then glance at the wall and see—based on the colored stickers and where the cards are placed—if any given programmer pair is ahead of or behind schedule. Those who are ahead of schedule can then easily find people who may be behind schedule and offer to give them some assistance. **This system requires no managers and no boring project status update meetings. It doesn't even require email**. In fact, Menlo employees rarely email each other, using it mostly for communicating with clients. And meetings are accomplished easily since everyone works in the same room. If a pair working on quality needs to talk to the project team about some particular results, they simply have to say the name of the team out loud. When the team responds, the meeting has started. Even their morning all-staff meetings take no more than 15 minutes as each pair simply states what they are working on that day. Immediately after the all-staff meeting, smaller groups form based on questions people have or connections that need to be made now that everyone knows what everyone else is working on. In short, when everything is made visible, the employees start making better decisions about how to get the work done, without requiring any actual layers of management. **Clarity, not management oversight and control, gives you better decisions.**

They bring clients into their systems

Menlo's commitment to clarity doesn't stop with its employees. Its clients actually have a window into all this transparency as well. On a weekly basis, clients come into the office and actually help make the decisions of what gets worked on and what doesn't. The programmers have written down all the tasks that they could be working on for a given project (including an estimate of how many hours each will take, denoted by the size of the card for that task), and those cards are then arranged by the client based on how much time its particular budget allows in a given week. Cards that get into the approved plan for the week will be worked on, and any card that is not in that plan won't. No surprises. Clients also get a weekly "show and tell" from the project team so they are aware of the results of the work, which then informs their next choices about work priorities for the next week.

For many organizations, having the client, customer, or sponsor integrally involved with weekly decision making around project management sounds like a nightmare. Traditional management assumes that decisions should always be placed in the hands of the experts who are best equipped to make those decisions, and given that customers are, by definition, less informed about the work that is done inside the organization, it seems logical to exclude them from the decisions the organization makes about getting work done.

> Our organization is very interested in external transparency—enough so [that] we have a review committee that takes into account who we sponsor and who we accept money from. This committee turned down $1 million from a sponsor because we felt the sponsor company didn't embody our mission.
>
> —*Millennial, b. 1987*

Unfortunately, that logic works better in theory than in practice, because the practice is more complex. In Menlo's case, the customer actually knows much more than Menlo does about certain aspects of the project, and those aspects should have weight in decision making. By leveraging clarity and showing the customer details about the tasks and how long they are estimated to take, combined with the weekly show and tell of the results, the customer ends up bringing in the right pieces of its internal picture to the decision-making process. The customers don't tell Menlo programmers how to write the code, and they don't have the authority to demand particular work be done faster than the programmers estimate it will take. So, their decision-making authority is limited. **But, by creating a system where more is visible—to everyone—it becomes easier to parse out decisions in a collaborative way, in which everyone's relative expertise is accounted for in sharing the decision-making load.**

> The company is 100 percent transparent. We as employees are aware of the funds, company goals, current changes, upcoming changes, all the way into the last funny thing said by our CEO's youngest child. [We're] all about running as a unit and being truthful and direct.
>
> —*Millennial, b. 1984*

Takeaways: Make Your Organization Clear

At some point in this chapter, you probably said to yourself something like "Yeah, but my organization isn't like Menlo Innovations, so that would never work here." You probably started off reading with interest about the idea of introducing more clarity into your organization and improving the quality of your decisions, but, by the time you got to the part where the clients were coming into Menlo's office a couple of times per week to plan out hourly tasks, you might have given up on the idea.

Don't give up hope. You don't have to be like Menlo to embrace clarity. That doesn't mean you can't use some of its techniques, modified to fit your context, of course. (The two of us actually use a version of Menlo's project-planning game in our own consulting company, Culture That Works.) The way Menlo staff write things down for everyone to see before, during, and after the work is done could definitely be applied somewhere within just about any organization, of any size, in any industry. But, in the end, it's not about the practices. It's about the culture. To help you figure this out, here are some recommendations.

Define Your Company Culture

Just like Digital, Clear is something you embed in your culture. The specific practices are an important part of that, but if you focus exclusively on these practices and processes, particularly ones that were developed and applied in a culture that is different from yours, then you will quickly be disappointed. And despite the popular opinion that culture is something very difficult to understand and even harder to change, plenty of companies make significant shifts to their cultures over a period of months, not years. A complete transformation of a large enterprise? Yes, that will take some time. But figuring out how to embed clarity into your culture to enable smarter decision making? That is within your reach.

Culture, at its essence, is about what is truly valued inside an organization. Culture is then expressed inside organizations through the words they use but, more importantly, through their actions and their internal processes.

Here's our official definition—feel free to stick this on your office wall:

Organizational culture is the collection of words, actions, thoughts, and "stuff" that clarifies and reinforces what a company truly values.[36]

It's all of that—from what you say your culture is in your literature, down to the underlying beliefs, attitudes, and habits that may even be hard for you to see any more, since they are so ingrained. Most importantly, though, culture comes alive through the way people work together. And a strong culture is one that can make a direct connection between what is truly valued and what specifically drives the success of the enterprise. You don't value things just because they sound nice. You value them because they work. That's your challenge here.

Where can having more clarity have the biggest impact on your success, and then how do you need to do things differently in order to get those results?

In the end, the answers will be unique to you and your organization. Rich Sheridan at Menlo figured out that introducing radical clarity in the project management process, in which nothing happened unless it was handwritten on an index card, would have an incredible impact on the quality of the software being written, the efficiency of the organization, and the engagement of his employees.

Another organization we worked with identified something completely different. It is a small government contractor that needed to successfully work both inside and outside of a large agency, and the staff realized that the core value of "having each other's back" was critical to maintaining the ongoing delicate balance that was necessary for success in the company's context. That meant the staff invested much more of their attention on working through conflicts, ensuring there was open communication, and standing by each other more consistently. They actually hired and fired based on these criteria.

The point is, your culture will be unique to your context. Do the work to figure this out, because even if you choose not to define it, the system will define it for you, and accidental, default cultures are rarely the most powerful ones. **Is your culture by design, or by default? You decide.**

Review Your Decision-Making Process

The purpose of clarity is to enhance decision making. When the right people have the right information in hand, they make the right decisions. The challenge, of course, is trying to figure out how to dial up the maximum amount of "right" in that sentence. And perhaps the bigger challenge is that the dominant mode of management for the last 100 years has told us (incorrectly) that maximizing decision making was a matter of control, expertise, and coordination. The organizational chart represents a decision-making flow chart, where harder decisions are pushed up to the more senior (and presumably more expert) managers. Then meetings are used to ensure decisions are coordinated, and, where senior people do not make the decisions, they are still held accountable for them, so in addition to making decisions they are required to "oversee" them somehow.

> I was told by another employee who had been with the company for a long time that salaries were all frozen across the board. This is not something publicly known in the office and was not ever disclosed to me by management. I think if a company is having financial struggles, that is definitely something they should be sharing with the employees.
> —*Millennial, b. 1984*

Is this an optimal system? Frankly, most organizations have no idea, because they do not systematically study the effectiveness of their decision making. Overall results are evaluated, certainly, and sometimes the results are attributed to decisions (particularly big, strategic decisions), but the truth is that your organization runs on a dynamic and flowing chain of decisions that are made constantly by every one of your employees on a daily basis. **It's not enough to look at only the big decisions. You have to look at the whole system.**

Assess the process

Marcia Blenko, Michael Mankins, and Paul Rogers from the consulting firm Bain and Company have developed an organizational decision-making assessment for large organizations.[37] The assessment evaluates decision making on four aspects:

- **Quality**. How good are the decisions that are made, and do they work out well?
- **Speed**. Can you make decisions faster than your competitors?
- **Yield**. How many of the decisions actually get converted to action?
- **Effort**. How much effort goes into making the decisions?

Their research found that the first three aspects of organizational decision making (quality, speed, and yield) were strongly correlated with better financial performance. The fourth aspect (effort) was not correlated as highly but did prove to be a drag on the benefits provided by the other three. In other words, if your organization makes high-quality decisions quickly that are frequently converted into action, but there are a great number of hoops to jump through and committees to meet with before the decisions get made, this "effort tax" means your overall performance won't be as high as it would be without the tax. If you work for a very large organization, Bain and Company offers an assessment that is tied into a database of benchmark responses from other large organizations so you can see how you compare.

How does your organization's decision-making system rate? When we do this work with smaller organizations, we gather a cross-functional group of key staff and have them each review the decisions they made over the last six months. We have them break down decisions by frequency—major decisions that are not made that often versus ongoing, regular decisions made frequently—and then within those two categories, group the decisions based on importance, or how critical they are to the success of the organization.

We then facilitate a group conversation to dig into the company's important decisions (both the big ones and the little ones) and evaluate how well they are doing along similar criteria. **The goal here is not to narrow** down the conversation down to a single conclusion about whether an organization is "good" or "bad" at decision making. It is about getting at a more nuanced understanding of the decision-making system inside the organization. You can do this, too, by looking for patterns around quality and yield, for example. Are certain departments or levels in the organization doing a better job with their decisions? Explore that in more detail to uncover the elements of your culture that impact your decisions.

> External transparency is absolutely necessary due to the public nature of the organization. Central decisions are not internally transparent; for example, the vision of our leaders is not necessarily communicated well or understood in terms of how everyday business is affected. At lower levels, different cultures reflect the level of transparency experienced.
> —*Millennial, b. 1984*

At that point, you should be able to introduce clarity into the conversation:

- Where can transparency enhance the decision making of the organization?

- Are some decisions less effective or slower because the people making them do not have the right information at the right time?

This kind of analysis will give you insight into where the capacity for clarity needs to be strengthened in your organization. **Clarity gives you better decisions.**

Enable the front line

One of the key insights that has driven Menlo Innovations' success as a software company is the awareness of a gap that exists in the traditional software design process that separates the software designers and the end users. That is, designers spend most of their time understanding the software and not enough time understanding the experience of actual users—and not just their experience using the software, but all of their experiences that are related to the use of the software, as well.

To bridge this gap, Menlo uses its high-tech anthropologists, who spend most of their time out of the office. They observe users in their natural working environments, learning about who they are, how they think, and what matters to them. That information ends up informing key decisions that are made in the software design process—decisions that would not have been as effective without that rich, contextual information. In designing a software system for an office within a county government, for example, they included screen-saver images of idyllic beach scenes, because they had noticed the employees often had postcards of such images on their cube walls (to reduce the stress of dealing with unhappy citizens concerning the county bureaucracy). Menlo designed systems and processes that enabled that kind of information to be in the hands of the decision makers—those writing the software code.[38]

Design a Transparency Architecture

To raise the bar in terms of clarity inside your organization, use the insights from your decision-making analysis to create an intentional system of information sharing that will lead to better decisions. Regardless of where you are in the organization, you can start by asking questions about transparency and access to more information, just like we did in our research. We asked our Millennial interviewees, "How is your organization responding to changing expectations around transparency (both internal and external) in today's business world?" You'll notice that this question very consciously assumes that expectations of transparency are changing (which they are), but it is not loaded or negative. We ask, "How are you responding?" not, "Why do your processes still suck?"—because the former will encourage proactive "action" answers.

In *Humanize*, we wrote about a financial planning organization[39] that built a system to make sure the right information from its national headquarters made it out to the branches so representatives could better answer customers' questions. It called the system a "transparency architecture," and, once it was in place, the organization saw its turnover rates among branch employees drop from 22 percent to 11 percent.

What would a transparency architecture look like in your organization? The answer will be unique to your situation, but here are some recommendations to get you started.

Share all the data

The most obvious area to look at for your transparency architecture is sharing data electronically with all parts of the system. This is the digital age, so find ways to ensure that basic data about the organization is accessible electronically to those who need it. As we mentioned above, financial data is often an area where increased data sharing can lead to better decisions. Employees at Morning Star, the tomato processing company, make their own decisions about purchasing equipment specifically because each team has a clear understanding of its own profitability. But don't stop with financial data. Can you share information from users and customers, like the Menlo high-tech anthropologists do? And if you have access to it, can you share insights from the analysis of "big data" with the right parts of the information? Also consider these questions about data sharing:

- Where is data stored?
- How is data organized?
- Where can you share more internal data?
- Where can you share more external data?
- How can you provide analysis and insights related to data?

We hold more meetings, but only include who needs to be there for the specific project so that way the people who need the information can get it. We also have a public drive where everyone can share their information and projects on one server to know what everyone is working on, and we have regular department meetings once a month to go over everyone's to-do list. Every employee has access to the budget and strategic plan and other executive documentation so everyone is on the same page at the organization.

—*Millennial, b. 1989*

Be clear about who decides

Getting the right information to people to help them make decisions should be one part of your transparency architecture, but an equally important component is making sure the whole organization is clear on exactly how decisions get made.

- Who makes which decisions?
- Who needs to sign off on them, and who needs to provide input on them?

Lack of clarity on these issues is frequently a huge inhibitor to good decisions. A memo from a senior executive at Yahoo in 2006 complained:

> *There are so many people in charge (or who believe they are in charge) that it's not clear if anyone is in charge.*[40]

Spend the time to draw some lines about who does what, and then ensure that those decision-making rules are made available to everyone in the organization.

Give access by default

Alongside who decides, a key piece of your transparency architecture is a clear understanding of who has access—to whom and to what data—inside your organization. In highly centralized systems, access tends to be controlled more tightly. Only certain people can approach other people with questions or requests for information, and it is often limited by the hierarchy. In more decentralized systems, people aren't as restricted, For example, at Happy State Bank (see Chapter 6), employees know they can call their most senior leaders—even the CEO—whenever they need to. And even with 600 employees, the CEO will get your name right and probably know to ask about how your kids did at the game last week. There is not one right way to do it, but restrictions on access bring with them restrictions on information flow, so make sure your access rules are consistent with the needs of your transparency architecture.

From Clear to Fluid

Let's recap where we are so far. We've established that Millennials have arrived in the workforce with the expectation (or hope) that their digital needs will be met: the right technologies, a focus on the user both internally and externally, and the ability to learn and innovate. From there, they know that, to do their jobs well, they should be able to find the information they need at their fingertips inside their organizations, just like they do at the flick of a finger across the smartphones in their pockets. They will feel frustrated if they don't have access to the knowledge they feel they need to execute on decisions; they will be stymied by red tape and bureaucracy. They'll wonder why the role of management is to block action—and they'll take steps to change that.

What would you do if you were in a position to remove the red tape? Let's talk Fluid.

;)

5. Fluid

When Jason Stirman was managing a team on the staff at Twitter, he was frustrated with the results he got by following the traditional management best practices. Management textbooks and even his mentors all advised him to insulate his direct reports from things in order to let them focus more productively on their work, but he found this approach backfired. "They just got angry, and confused, and disconnected," Stirman explained. "I was constantly censoring all this information, and they were happier when they knew everything."[41] He also found that he got better results in managing conflict among his staff by simply encouraging people to get to know each other better. Once the relationships started being built, his people ended up resolving their conflicts on their own.

This was a conflict that literally kept me up at night, and as soon as there was space for them to connect as people, it was fixed.[42]

A few years later, Stirman moved from Twitter to a new company founded by Twitter co-founder Ev Williams called Medium, where he continued his experiments in new ways of managing. This time, Stirman and his colleagues at Medium went deeper by embracing an experimental new management system called Holacracy. Holacracy is a system for leading and managing organizations that deviates significantly from traditional organizational structures. Instead of static lines and boxes to depict authority relationships, it organizes around more fluid sets of circles and processes designed for continuous improvement. It has been described as an "operating system" for the organization, allowing a company to grow and develop in a more organic way, giving more people in the organization the power to make decisions and solve relevant problems.

Holacracy is the product of a series of experiments conducted by Brian Robertson and his colleagues at Ternary Software, a company that Robertson created with the express intention of finding a better way to run organizations. His quest was rooted in an experience that is all too common in organizations: the feeling that, despite knowing that our current approach to work is sub-optimal, we seem unable to actually move the needle and change things. Robertson wanted to create a concrete and replicable system that would remove the obstacles that prevent us from making work better.

Robertson's initial experiments focused on building the company culture in ways that should sound fairly familiar: creating core values, seeking to empower people, and emphasizing learning and development. He and his colleagues then started to integrate the principles from agile software development into the organization, leveraging its focus on self-organizing teams, transparency, and adaptive planning and responding. They also studied a number of different collaborative decision-making processes, including one used at a Dutch company in the 1970s under the name of "sociocracy," the initial inspiration for the name Holacracy.

But none of the individual experiments captured all the right elements. They knew that the traditional command-and-control systems, in which bosses and managers controlled and dictated the work, were not as effective as the agile software design practices that they were implementing, but the purely decentralized and collaborative models also felt lacking, often leading to what they described as the slow and painful "tyranny of consensus." **A key breakthrough in the design of the Holacracy model was the idea that authority should be distributed in a set of roles, rather than a hierarchy of people, which would enable the decentralized system to stay on track with the needs of the organization**. As problems or "tensions" in the system are identified, the Holacracy system enables people with expertise relevant to particular problems to quickly get the authority they need to start solving them.

This is just the kind of system that Stirman and his colleagues at Medium were looking for. Holacracy helps them to create circles of self-organized employees who need to work together to get things done. Everything is explicit, so there is no confusion about who holds what role and has what authority. According to Stirman, the system helps them to be faster and more agile:

> *You don't have to wait for everyone up a ladder to sign off. This can take weeks or months, when Holacracy says, "You know what, we're going to hire the best people we know and trust them to make decisions for us." All day people make decisions, own parts of the company, and act on them. The momentum this creates far outweighs someone making a bad decision. You also have the momentum to change course quickly.*[43]

And it's more than just tech startups that are buying into this decentralized system. In 2014, the online retailer Zappos embraced Holacracy. Zappos has 1,500 employees, which will be organized into roughly 400 circles under the new system (which won't be completely rolled out until after this book goes to print, so we'll be interested to see how it plays out). Some doubt that the system can be scaled to that level, and indeed it's the largest organization to use the Holacracy system to date.

What Is Fluid?

The extent to which Zappos' Holacracy implementation succeeds or fails is actually only a side-story in the bigger narrative that is unfolding in management regarding the transformation of hierarchies in organizations today. Management was invented in the late 19th and early 20th centuries primarily to deal with one issue: scale. When your economy consists mostly of scattered towns populated by farmers and local businesses owned by individuals and families, you don't really need "management" as we know it today. But, as we entered the industrial age, our economy required larger groups of people to come together to produce large quantities of goods and services. To achieve this scale, we needed management, and specifically hierarchy. The very first organizational charts date back to the late 1800s, coming out of the railroad industry. To manage an enterprise at that scale, the whole system had to know who was responsible for what—who would send telegrams to whom about where the tracks were down and what would be done with that information, for example. Without a structure defining this, the system would remain dangerously inefficient.

And so the bureaucracy was born. Despite the resulting efficiency, it did not take us long to start hating our hierarchies. The term "bureaucracy" was coined in the late 19th century, referring primarily to government offices, but it always had a pejorative undertone. Our productivity and efficiency were increasing, but so was our frustration with various aspects of bureaucracy, like individual departments or managers trying to consolidate power over their "fiefdoms" or blind adherence to policies and procedures that had outlived their usefulness. We struggled to cut through bureaucracy's "red tape," and we shook our heads as technical experts were unsuccessfully thrust into management positions, simply because it is the only way they could advance in the organization. We've built an incredible global economy over the last century, but some argue that the cost—the negative aspects of bureaucracy—may be outweighing the benefits. In a *Fortune* blog post, management author Gary Hamel declares that "bureaucracy must die" because it creates friction, discourages dissent, hobbles initiative, and thwarts innovation.[44]

So, does Holacracy mark the end of hierarchy in management? Not exactly. While Hamel's points about the problems of bureaucracy should indeed be addressed, we will never get rid of hierarchy altogether. **In addition to efficiency and coordination, hierarchies in all human systems provide a key benefit that we simply cannot live without: They reduce cognitive load.** One of the primary values of hierarchies is the way they predetermine certain aspects of our organizational lives. They declare ahead of time who gets to make certain decisions, and they even determine things like who gets to talk or where people sit in certain circumstances. As a result, we can take those things off of our list of things to be thinking about as we do our work, and that makes life easier for everyone. Studies have shown that while people have a generally negative view of hierarchies, they also indicate that they are "happier, calmer, and more productive when power and status differences are present and well understood."[45]

The more we have on our mental plates (our cognitive load), the harder it is to get our work done. Hierarchies reduce that load for us. So, our desire to do away with hierarchy is ultimately misguided, as the benefits that come from resolving bureaucratic frustrations can be outweighed by new problems caused by increased cognitive load.

Fluid Hierarchies

The solution is to create a hierarchy that is flatter and more fluid. A flat hierarchy may sound like an oxymoron, but remember that a hierarchy is simply a system for distributing authority—different people end up having more authority than others over certain decisions. **But maintaining distributed authority does not necessarily require the very vertical nature of traditional management hierarchy**. Vertical hierarchies consolidate decision-making authority in a cascading structure of managers. The higher you go in the structure, the more authority you have, narrowing to a single person at the top. This reduces cognitive load, since we can keep track of a relatively small number of people who are "in charge," and most people consider it the best way to ensure that everyone in the system can be held accountable. It seems impossible to flatten these hierarchies, because it would simply mean adding more people to each layer, which defeats the purpose of clarifying who's in charge and makes accountability messier.

That's true, but only because we assume that a hierarchy has to be static. Management hierarchies were invented in a simpler time. Railroad tracks don't move. You could design a decision-making structure for managing track work at a single point in time and safely expect it to work the same way for years to come, because the tracks don't change. We scaled operations of many types of organizations very quickly using this approach, so it has always been a given that organizations could design a complete decision-making authority structure and expect it to work as it was designed every time, in every context. It turns out that our hierarchies' inflexibility is actually what requires the vertical design. When you paint that single picture of authority at one point in time, you must force-fit the authority into manageable pieces. A static hierarchy needs to be vertical to work properly. Those two aspects go hand in hand.

But in the internet age, nothing is static.

> We never had a traditional structure but have continued to trend towards a holocratic organization at the VC level. That does not mean all information is known by all parties, but rather it means that people are informed and empowered to consider, analyze, and determine action on initiatives in which they have direct involvement and to stay out of the way or remain unfocused on issues in which they would have limited knowledge in the first place. On an entity level, individual leaders determine the structure that works best for their business.
>
> —*Millennial, b. 1987*

Change Is the Only Constant

We all recognize that the pace of change has gone through the roof and that disruption is the norm now, so why are we relying on static, inflexible, and thus vertical hierarchies? Before the internet, you could count your credible sources for "news" on one hand, but during the 2006 coup in Thailand, an important source for photographic journalism came from a "fashion-obsessed college student going by the name gnarlykitty."[46] Gnarlykitty did not have journalistic credentials, but, at that particular moment in time, CNN was being blacked out in Thailand, so amateur news sources became the best sources for information. In the internet age, the definition of "news source" varies depending on the context, rather than being the same all the time. Expertise can be validated today via the social internet, rather than exclusively by someone higher up in the chain.

Circles, Not Pyramids

The whole point of a system like Holacracy is to break out of that static mold. The system organizes people into circles based on the work they do and their domains of expertise and then institutes disciplined processes by which people in those circles can identify and resolve "tensions" based on gaps between reality and the ideal. There are separate processes to deal with operational tensions (working in the business) and governance tensions (working on the business). This doesn't make everyone equal or do away with hierarchy. The founders at Medium have designed the circles in a way that gives them decision-making authority that others don't have, and as long as that continues to help the business move forward, that's fine. Ev Williams, the founder of Medium, is the sole person occupying the role of "product strategy," so he decides which features go public, but there are circles of people who make decisions about which ideas get prototyped and built. The Holacracy system is designed to help everyone at Medium figure out if that way of doing it is holding them back, and if it is they can change it.

It is not the absence of hierarchy or the uniformity of decision-making authority that makes an organization fluid. It is the ability to shift and morph those things in the service of accomplishing more.

In our organization, we began utilizing circles, which are essentially groups of 4 to 6 people assigned to an initiative. The leaders of these circles are given full decision-making power, and they could be any level within our organization.

—*Millennial, b. 1986*

Why Millennials Care About Fluid

As we pointed out in Chapter 2, the Millennial generation grew up with "blurred lines" around authority and hierarchy, as their parents were very much an active part of their lives. As they enter the workforce, they are expecting a different role in the hierarchy. As one Millennial we surveyed put it:

> *I do not feel like the top-down approach will be an effective leadership strategy moving forward. That worked with the Baby Boomers, but it can definitely not work with us. Our generation is different and we want to feel like we have a voice at the organization that we work for.*

Of course, sentiments like these may sound familiar, as younger generations throughout history have expressed frustration about their experience at the bottom of the hierarchy when they enter the workforce. Millennials, however, have a distinct focus on the shifting and dynamic (i.e., fluid) nature of authority in organizations:

> *I have found personally that if I want to see something happen or for us to move forward in an area, I can't always wait for or rely on a more senior staff person to come up with the idea, so sometimes I have to step out and call a meeting together to get the ball rolling and get people talking.*

> *You become a leader when you have the most experience or knowledge, not necessarily the tenure or age.*

Today's work is being performed in teams, so the top-down approach is slowly fading. The team approach is best because it allows the team to delegate responsibilities to individuals based on their expertise.

A fluid hierarchy learns how to shift decision-making authority and action to the individuals and groups who are best equipped to be successful given the context. This often means shifting power to those who have best access to information or are closest to the customer, rather than always relying on senior managers at headquarters who have experience and tenure but maybe not the context-specific information or perspective necessary to take the right action at the right time. In traditional vertical hierarchies, thinking and analysis is frequently separated from action. Generally speaking, the managers do the thinking and the direct reports are expected to take the actions. This approach works only in a very static environment.

In other words, it does not work today and will never make sense to Millennials.

What Fluid Looks Like

Of course, the Holacracy operating system is not the only way to achieve a fluid hierarchy. You simply have to build into your culture the right combination of processes and access that will allow more fluidity and effectiveness in your decision making.

> We're in a very unique atmosphere, filled with Millennials who all have interesting ideas and work styles. Our leaders are all focused on allowing team members to lead their own projects that help fulfill our company goals, which allows everyone to be responsible for the success of our company.
>
> —Millennial, b. 1988

One of the more famous examples of a fluid company in today's business press is the Morning Star tomato processing company. It was featured in a cover story in *Harvard Business Review* at the end of 2011 and has since been the focus attention from *Inc.* magazine and the Drucker Institute, among others. Morning Star is a particularly compelling story for fluidity, given that it is not some small Silicon Valley startup. Morning Star is a tomato processing company with factories and trucks and farms. Yet it has no managers, and every single employee, including seasonal workers, has the authority to purchase whatever equipment he or she needs to get the job done. This is a $700 million-per-year business, with as many as 2,400 employees during the peak season, and not a single one of those employees needs approval to make a purchase.

We heard a Morning Star employee tell a story of one of those purchases that he made back when he was a seasonal employee. He had determined that having a laptop setup at a particular area where he was working would allow for some real-time data to be collected and displayed to the relevant people, resulting in increased efficiency. He didn't need approval, so he spent the $1,500 and ran the experiment. It turns out his predictions were correct, and when other teams learned of the cost savings, they started implementing his ideas throughout the system, saving the company more than $100,000 per year.

For this to work, though, each team needs to understand its own profitability. Morning Star will actually pay employees to go to basic accounting classes, because the system relies on their financial acumen.[47] When the capacity to understand profitability is shared more broadly among employees, then it makes sense to distribute that decision-making authority, rather than consolidate it among managers. Morning Star also relies heavily on employees to clarify how they work with each other. Everyone writes a "Colleague Letter of Understanding," or CLOU, that negotiates expectations with every other employee that his or her work impacts. Performance metrics are handled in these documents, negotiated by the actual people who will be meeting them. Basing these conversations in reality, according to Morning Star, makes them more effective.[48]

The essence of a fluid hierarchy is a refined understanding of how a group of people can most effectively get done what needs to get done. That was the basis of the original Holacracy experiments: what gets in the way of being able to sense the tensions and resolve them quickly. Morning Star shifted its focus to individual teams and units and developed new practices that would enable the teams to manage themselves, and it has had double-digit growth with effectively zero turnover.[49] Once you accept the idea that "managers" are not as inherently valuable as we have been made to believe our whole lives, all sorts of opportunities open up to do things differently.

Today's work is being performed in teams, so the top-down approach is slowly fading. The team approach is best because it allows the team to delegate responsibilities to individuals based on their expertise. The days of the boss telling you what to do are over ... to a certain extent. Now everyone has the opportunity to serve as a leader of a team or project, and this makes you feel like you are really contributing to the overall success of the organization and provides you with a sense of ownership. I do not feel like the top-down approach will be an effective leadership strategy moving forward. That worked with the Baby Boomers, but it definitely cannot work with us. Our generation is different and we want to feel like we have a voice at the organization that we work for. Hierarchies are definitely shifting. It's no longer top-down but more lateral. Everyone is equal when you are in a team setting; however, it is understood that there is one person responsible for managing the project, but it takes the work of the entire team in order for the project to be successful.

–Millennial, b. 1984

Case Study: Quality Living, Inc.

Quality Living, Inc. (QLI) is a company in Omaha, Nebraska, that provides rehabilitation services to individuals with brain and spinal cord injuries. This is not easy work. Its patients have had their lives shattered, and the recovery process is painful and challenging. Services are provided in QLI's residential campus where it has 350 employees, including various kinds of medical specialists (speech therapists, physical therapists, occupational therapists, etc.) and a range of staff who manage the functions in the residential facilities and support the patients in rebuilding their lives.

If you look at QLI's website, you can piece together a fairly traditional-looking organizational chart. Its five-person executive team includes a president and four vice presidents. There are seven different clinical directors, covering areas like psychology, nursing, and nutrition. There's a marketing and development team and a number of service coordinators. At first glance, this doesn't look like a radically flat or particularly fluid hierarchy.

But when you take a closer look at how QLI runs its operations, a different picture emerges. Recently, a clinical meeting took place on campus that included a broad range of employees, including the CEO, some director-level staff, some therapists, and some residential staff. At this particular meeting, there also happened to be two psychology interns who were relatively new to the organization. After the meeting, one of the staff asked the interns if they had realized that the CEO was one of the participants in the meeting. No one had been introduced by title, so the interns were unaware of the CEO's presence, and when they were asked to guess which one of the meeting participants was the CEO, they both guessed incorrectly.

They create power flux

There are not many organizations where the CEO's presence would not be immediately detected and identified by strangers. Even in the absence of titles and name tags, you would be able to sense the deference to her ultimate authority, a likely hesitance for others to share too much or take up too much air time. The CEO's presence typically generates an unspoken, civilian version of the "ten-HUT" you hear when a military officer walks into the room. That doesn't happen at QLI, obviously. That meeting was acutely focused on the issues and problems that needed to be solved, not on the hierarchical representation in the room. When the interns were asked who was leading the meeting, they picked the direct care staff person (a position fairly low on the organizational chart), because that was the person who was most vocal in the meeting.

That made sense in this case, because the specific clinical issues being discussed in that meeting put that direct care staff at the heart of the conversation. QLI's philosophy on culture and leadership grew out of a program called Mindsets,[50] which was developed by QLI's founding president and CEO, Dr. Kim Hoogeveen, and one of the mindsets central to his approach is called "power flux." Depending on what is going on, the person with the relevant expertise is in charge, and that fluctuates. In that meeting, the group identified dynamics in the residential facility as the key problems to be solved, so the house staff became in charge of the meeting, regardless of the formal power differential that existed in the room.

For "power flux" to work, though, QLI takes a disciplined and rigorous approach to understanding just what "relevant expertise" really means.

They balance their expertise

The healthcare field comes from a very hierarchical tradition, including ever-specializing divisions of expertise. Speech therapists, for example, have undertaken a specific course of study to go along with their clinical experience that was supervised by an expert in their field. Based on this expertise, they would obviously expect their diagnoses and treatment recommendations to be respected. **At QLI, that expertise is indeed respected, but it is balanced with other expertise, including a deep knowledge of the patient's life, the patient's values, and the patient's dreams and aspirations**. One of the clinicians teaches a class at the local university and finds that when he presents a patient case study, the students are quick to develop a treatment plan based only on the medical facts presented.

> *They didn't even ask one question about the patient—who they are and what makes them tick. Then we should go back and redo the treatment plan. In healthcare, this is the way we should be thinking, but we're not.*

One of the patients at QLI, for example, was a passionate longboard skateboarder before his spinal cord injury. The staff there took the time to get to know the patient well enough to discover this passion, so when they needed to work on some strength and balancing exercises with the patient, they got a longboard skateboard, removed the wheels, and used it in the therapy. The patient "lit up" when he realized the board would be a part of the therapy.

Another patient was passionate about scuba diving, so the staff found a local adaptive diving program that works with people with disabilities. Another patient does therapy through kayaking. All of these methods are nontraditional and in many contexts would require special approvals and exceptions from the policies and standard practices. **At QLI, when you know what matters to the patient at a deep level, that expertise gives you the authority to make decisions.** It's not that QLI staff discount the expertise that, say, a speech therapist brings to the patient and the treatment plan, but they recognize that the direct care staff, who is with the patient seven days a week, also has expertise that must be included when figuring out what to do. That gives the team the freedom they need to innovate.

There are no lines we can't cross in terms of creativity and what we can do for our residents.

They communicate well and thoughtfully

This approach is particularly motivating to younger staff. It was a Millennial employee who made the above statement about the facilitation of creativity.. And this is the generation that grew up with "blurred lines," so they expect to be able to interact with people across hierarchical lines when necessary. But that doesn't make it easy.

One of the key factors in making the fluid hierarchy work at QLI is the attention staff pay to internal communication in their culture. Senior staff make visible efforts to open up lines of communication and remain approachable, despite their titles. Within the culture there are discussions about another of Dr. Hoogeveen's Mindsets: the difference between a "cosmo" and a "local." Locals are the ideal: people who are humble, willing to help, and be a part of the community just like anyone else. Cosmos, on the other hand, are people who tie their ego to their title, accolades, or accomplishments. People are hired with this distinction in mind, and senior staff know that to be a local they must be approachable and curious about others in the community. According to a physical therapist at QLI:

People with power in the company would just talk to me, and ask me how I was. I would learn later that it was the CEO or a clinical director. Everything is flat.

They teach communication skills

QLI also recognizes that the open communication required in a fluid hierarchy can be stifled if the staff cannot handle conflict. They provide training in conflict resolution to employees and talk frequently about the need for "friendly friction." They work on learning how to disagree without it damaging the workplace relationship, and they constantly pay attention to getting more voices in the conversation when the decisions get tougher. All of this is deeply embedded in their culture, which is supported by two specific roles: the mentor and the professional. Representing about 5 percent and 1 percent of the employees in the company, respectively, mentors and professionals can come from any level of the hierarchy, and they work explicitly to reinforce and support the culture, particularly around communication. Employees are encouraged to seek them out for support, and they pay attention to people who might be struggling and then coach them to get them back on track.

I have seen in the last few years (some due to our current staff size and mix) a much more collaborative environment where any of us can propose and take the lead on a project. I have found personally that if I want to see something happen or for us to move forward in an area, I can't always wait for or rely on a more senior staff person to come up with or propose the idea, so sometimes I have to step out and call a meeting together to get the ball rolling and get people talking. I think that's a very "Millennial" trait; we want to see change and progress happen, and, if we don't see it, we don't hesitate to take matters into our own hands. I would venture to say that Millennials value and desire a workplace where they have the ability and autonomy to propose and run with new ideas and also have coaching and more senior expertise along the way. Those are the organizations that will attract and retain Millennials.

—Millennial, b. 1989

Takeaways: Make Your Organization Fluid

As you can see, maintaining a fluid hierarchy takes some effort, though in QLI's case it is obviously worth that effort. Its system of fluid decision making generates positive results for both employees and customers. A full 100 percent of its customers (clients, families, and payors) say they would recommend QLI to a loved one, a testament to the quality solutions that QLI comes up with by letting those who know more about the patient's situation to be involved in the decision making. Internally, 95 percent of its employees participated in its most recent culture survey, and average scores in every single category were above 7 on a 9-point scale. (Pride was 8.5.) Its turnover rate is well below average for healthcare companies, never getting above 28 percent per year over a 20-year period, and, even then, most of those transitions were employees who were not a good fit for the company culture, which QLI considers "positive turnover." Its negative turnover numbers—the people who leave who QLI would want to keep—has been below 10 percent annually throughout its history. At the heart of these results is QLI's investment **in a culture that allows authority to be fluid and**

enables better decision making through effective conflict conversations and being "crazy good at communication," as one employee put it.

When you look at the threads that connect QLI's experience with other companies that have unlocked the potential of a fluid hierarchy (like Morning Star or Zappos), you will see that two fundamental building blocks can enable such a system in your organization: understanding what drives success and investing in soft skills.

Understand What Drives Success

This may sound like an issue of strategy rather than organizational culture or structure, but it's important to remember that there are different levels to understanding what drives the success of your organization. At a high level, every company understands its success drivers, or it obviously wouldn't still be around. That's the basic strategic level, where you get clear on where your company is going to compete and how you will win with your particular set of products and services. QLI provides rehabilitation services to people with brain and spinal cord injuries, so its high-level success drivers revolve around providing high-quality medical care to patients. At a high level, it doesn't need to be fluid. QLI could hire the best-trained physical therapists, speech therapists, and so on and put them into a rigid, vertical hierarchy and still provide high-quality healthcare. But there is more to understanding what drives its success—the deep connection its front line staff have with patients.

Find your true mission

At QLI, high-quality healthcare is a given, but from the very beginning QLI staff realized that they were not just dealing with patients who had healthcare issues; they were dealing with people whose lives had been shattered. Rebuilding a shattered life requires more than medical attention. It requires a deep knowledge of the patient as a person and integrating that person's life and passions into the medical care. It is that kind of intimacy with the patient that requires a flatter hierarchy, where more people know more about all facets of the patient's life. **QLI does not choose to be fluid because it is a cool new management technique. It chooses to be fluid because that makes it more successful.**

We are extremely collaborative. Helping to further break down silos here allows us to be more nimble and keep a smaller staff rather than needing to bulk up for individual department needs. I think the top-down approach is also changing because many leaders (actual organization leaders) are starting to think through how to deal, interact, and do business with Millennials in the coming years, and so they are working with lower-tier staff on strategy unlike in the past. I don't think this trend will change for some time.

—Millennial, b. 1986

Think beyond the profit margin

Take Zappos as another example. At a high level, all it does is sell shoes and other apparel online, so its success could be driven by solid logistics, good relationships with manufacturers, and effective marketing. But early on, Zappos figured out that giving the customer a "wow" experience is actually at the heart of its success. That is number one on its internal list of core values. Why? Because selling shoes online seems like an impossible situation, given that we assume we must first try shoes on before we buy them. The heart of success for Zappos, therefore, can't simply be about providing the opportunity to buy shoes; we already have that at shoe stores. Zappos realized that it needed to draw people in with not just good customer service, but customer service that would blow people away. The kind of customer service where customers hang up the phone, and literally say "wow" out loud.

Understanding success at that level has implications for the culture at Zappos, particularly around being flat and fluid. Even before it adopted Holacracy, Zappos had a decentralized culture, specifically because of its deep clarity about what drives its success. To provide a "wow" experience, it had to give more power to people at the lowest levels of the hierarchy, the call-center employees, because they were closest to the customer. Zappos call-center employees make their own decisions about whether or not to upgrade a customer's account or give them free shipping. They are famous, in fact, for being able to stay on the phone as long as they want with customers. (The record is more than 11 hours with a single customer.) That is not a best practice in the call-center industry, whose typical metrics focus on the efficiency of getting customers on and off the phone as quickly as possible. But at Zappos you need to wow the customer, so the staff stay decentralized, even if it's not efficient. Note that, despite this inefficiency, Zappos managed to grow from $1 million in sales to $1 billion in sales in just eight years.

Be proactive

We could try to scare you into being fluid. We could make a compelling case, actually, that the Millennial generation is going to storm into the workplace over the next several years and demand it. **But you won't access fluid's true power by being reactionary. You need to look more deeply at your organization and your business model to understand what drives success and clearly identify how being more fluid does or does not connect to that.** Given today's environment, we would be surprised to find organizations that would not benefit from the advantages of being fluid, but you still have to figure that out for yourself. When we do culture assessments with clients, we always include an in-depth, qualitative assessment designed to uncover this deeper level of what drives the success of the enterprise so that it can be connected to the culture-strengthening interventions.

Invest in Soft Skills

Once the deeper strategic connection is made, you still have to handle the implementation of a fluid hierarchy, and that's where so-called "soft" skills become critical. Remember that a rigid hierarchy does serve a purpose: reducing cognitive load. Over the years, we have learned to rely on hierarchy to determine things like who gets to decide and where the information flows, which allowed us to focus our attention on other aspects of running the organization. What we didn't realize, perhaps, is that by allowing the hierarchy to literally structure our relationships internally, we let our basic skills in building and maintaining relationships among the human beings in our organizations atrophy. That is probably why we considered these skills to be "soft" (less important) to begin with—the hierarchy was already taking care of it.

> Our exec team is accessible, fallible, and criticize-able—as in, they're real humans! Our internal social tool lets people loop upper levels of management into conversations and even challenge their ideas, and it's all visible to the rest of the company, so you know when they're not being responsive or giving shoddy answers. I had not experienced this before at previous organizations.
>
> —*Millennial, b. 1989*

Fluid hierarchies are more dynamic and flexible, which puts the onus back on the people in your organization to do a better job at managing their relationships. That is why QLI is "crazy good at communication" and provides training for staff in conflict resolution skills. That is why Zappos actually encourages its employees to be a little weird—authenticity is actually an important skill when it comes to relationship building. That's why Morning Star has all of its employees write up letters of understanding with each other—the shared understanding unlocks the potential of the fluid hierarchy. If you want a fluid hierarchy, then you need to build the internal capacity for effective relationship building in these areas.

Teach conflict resolution

The ability to confront and work through conflict, without the drama and angst that we typically associate with it, is at the heart of making a fluid hierarchy work. Conflict resolution has long been an underdeveloped skill inside organizations. In a command-and-control hierarchy, the primary directive is to follow orders, thus eliminating the need to actually resolve conflict. At best, one assumed that major conflicts were resolved at the level of senior management teams before the orders were handed down the chain, but in reality that rarely happened. In Patrick Lencioni's best-selling *Five Dysfunctions of a Team*[51] (written squarely about corporate senior management teams), the core dysfunction is a lack of trust, but immediately following is the inability to raise and resolve conflict.

The result has been a large-scale avoidance of conflict inside organizations. Since we're bad at it, the only experiences we have of conflict inside organizations tend to be the ugly ones, and that only reinforces our desire to avoid it. But in fluid hierarchies this doesn't work. **Where decision-making authority is more fluid, people throughout the structure will be forced to figure things out themselves, and that requires the smooth handling of conflict when it emerges.** Avoiding the conflict simply gives it space to get worse or more complicated.

Make sure your people know how to manage and resolve conflict. Training courses in conflict resolution should not be hard to find, but they should ideally include the following elements.

- *Interest-based problem solving.* The phrase "win-win" has almost become trite in the business lexicon these days, but it is based on some important principles that employees in fluid hierarchies need to know. We too often try to solve problems by advocating for our preferred solution and poking holes in the other side's stated answer. But, if we seek instead to understand the reasoning behind the other party's position, we are more likely to uncover some solutions neither of us had thought of that will actually meet both of our interests (a win-win). If you're going to handle conflict well, you need to be clear about whether or not your basic interests are in conflict in the first place, so help your staff develop the skills of inquiry and analysis that get to the roots rather than stay on the surface.

- *Emotional intelligence.* Whether we like it or not, human beings are emotional creatures, and our actual brain chemistry causes us to experience our emotions before we have a chance to think about them or pretend they are not there. At its core, emotional intelligence is about building skills in recognizing our own emotional reactivity and managing it in a way that it doesn't interfere with important conflict conversations.

- *Shared understanding.* One of the core skills for navigating conflict situations is being able to stay with the conversation down to the level where both parties can develop a shared understanding of key issues. This does not mean they need to agree, but they must understand each other and increase the amount of data available to make sense of what is happening. This is where most conflicts go awry to begin with; each side has a different view of the "reality" on which the conflict is based, and, because they don't explore the underlying data or assumptions that support that view, they go around in circles. We frequently use a tool called the Ladder of Inference[52] to provide teams with a reference point they can use to slow down the conversation and develop a more common understanding of the conflict. This paves the way for more effective problem-solving down the line.

- *Effective feedback.* Conflict situations invariably require the parties to give each other feedback, but traditional delivery mechanisms focus on judging the other person and demanding they change their ways to resolve the conflict. The bottom line is humans hate to be judged and told what to do. But, when feedback can be consistently delivered with a focus on specific and observable behaviors that are connected to negative impacts that the other party can understand, then the parties stand a much better chance at working out a new solution together.

There is more to conflict resolution than what's listed here (you can get a Ph.D. in conflict resolution if you so desire), but these basic building blocks should be enough to facilitate creating a more fluid hierarchy.

Ask for authenticity

Authenticity does not usually make the list of "soft skills" in your business training program catalogue. You are more likely to see topics like conflict resolution, communication, teamwork, collaboration, and even outliers like enthusiasm or resilience. (For the record, we are still puzzled about how you teach people to be enthusiastic, or why you would want to.) But, for a fluid organization, authenticity is a critical skill. **Authenticity involves moving through the world as your whole self, so that your external behavior and the way you engage with others is very closely aligned with**

your deeper identity, purpose, and even destiny. When the way you show up at work becomes disconnected from who you are inside, you are being inauthentic. Note, this is not about constant self-expression, as some critics of authenticity in the workplace assert. You can be authentic and still make choices about what parts of yourself to share in any given context, and that's fine. It's when workplace expectations cause you to behave in ways that are not true to who you are that problems emerge.

> I feel that things in my organization are very open-door policy. They understand and value each individual, and they know that the people that work here make the difference, so they do put a lot of thought in the hiring process and also in the learning part of each person's career path.
> —*Millennial, b. 1982*

Why does that matter to fluid organizations? Because fluid organizations intentionally spread power throughout the hierarchy. Fluid organizations rely on the individuals in the system to do the work of figuring out who makes decisions and why, rather than having the hierarchy decide that for them. Authenticity makes that constant negotiation easier by doing what the hierarchy used to do, reducing cognitive load. **When your people are confident that their coworkers are more consistently who they appear to be, it becomes easier to speak the truth, challenge each other, and tackle the tough issues**. You spend less of your time trying to figure out how people will react or how they expect you to behave in the first place. Both of you get to simply be who you are. More is put out on the table, and less is hidden behind the curtain, and that leaves more of your mental bandwidth for handling the job of making the flat hierarchy work.

Authenticity, however, is much more easily understood than practiced. Bonnie Ware spent years working in palliative care with people literally on their deathbeds. As these patients reflected on their lives, they expressed, as one might expect, some regrets about their choices. The number-one regret they expressed was about authenticity:

I wish I'd had the courage to live a life true to myself, not the life others expected of me.[53]

Here are some ways you can surface authenticity inside your organization.

- *Self awareness.* Personality assessments like the DISC profile or Myers-Briggs can help employees get clearer about their own preferences and styles, which is a good first step toward deeper self-awareness. If done in the context of a team or group, this can also be helpful in conflict resolution.

- *Life goals.* As diversity trainer and consultant Joe Gerstandt points out, if you want to act in ways that are consistent with your purpose and goals in life, then you need to have some clarity in that area to begin with.[54] While the ultimate responsibility for this work lies with the employee, the organization can facilitate the work through the annual performance-review process. Fitness Australia (the professional association for the fitness industry in Australia) has its employees complete "personal success plans" as part of the review process, which are solely and explicitly about the employees achieving their own destiny. They are not evaluated on the work, but employees share them on the intranet so they can support each other in achieving them. Our white paper *Making Performance Management Work*[55] contains detailed information about what Fitness Australia accomplished and how. Consider these questions:

  o How can you incorporate more information about your employees' personal drives and goals into your performance-review process?

  o How can you embed a feedback process that occurs more than just annually?

- *Community.* Authenticity has a yin-yang relationship with a strong community. The best communities are ones that allow people to be themselves fully, and authentic individuals typically create the strongest and most vibrant communities. Be intentional about what kind of community you have among your staff and strengthen it by facilitating connections and relationships and supporting community rituals and artifacts.

- o How can you provide space for people to share their goals with each other and surface ways they can help each other?
- o What are your community rituals, and how do they help create bonds?

True authenticity is not easy, and it's not common. The pressure is strong to conform in organizations and leave your true self at home, so supporting your employees to be more authentic will require some investment.

From Fluid to Fast

In this chapter, we looked at new models for internal hierarchies, such as the procedurally detailed new Holacracy model and the more porous QLI "power flux." These examples are important because they are starting to be implemented in well-known companies, they take into account the shifting nature of 21st-century work, and they rely on bringing more of our full selves to work. Who doesn't want that? But, for Millennials, it's not just about removing red tape and working better in collaborative groups; being able to come together for specific projects and then disband makes sense because it taps into a better, more networked, more fluid way of working.

At its best, becoming more Fluid enables action, productivity, and results. And along with Digital and Clear, it's the third piece of the puzzle that leads to what we're all trying to achieve.

All paths lead to Fast.

;)

6. Fast

In their last semester at the University of California Berkeley, Nikhil Arora and Alejandro Velez learned that it was possible to grow gourmet mushrooms using discarded coffee grounds. This was a relatively obscure fact, presented in their business ethics class during a discussion about sustainability, and given their career trajectories it probably should have remained irrelevant to them. Arora and Velez were business majors, and they had already lined up good jobs for themselves, Nikhil in consulting and Alejandro in investment banking in New York. Given the economy in 2010, those job offers were nothing to sneeze at, but for some reason the idea of turning waste into fresh, local food captured their attention. They went online and learned everything they could about the idea, and then started experimenting in Velez's fraternity house kitchen. Within a few months of first learning of the idea, they had secured a $5,000 grant from the university, declined their job offers, and started down the unlikely path of becoming mushroom farmers.

Four years later, sales revenue at their company, Back to the Roots, was approaching $5 million, and they had a staff of 15. They only had two products, but they were being carried by large, national retailers, which fueled the company's growth. And nearly every employee in the company is a Millennial. Arora and Velez are among the oldest employees, at 26 years old. According to Arora, the company is very flat and very entrepreneurial. Everyone has the freedom to explore new ways of doing things, and, as we mentioned back in Chapter 4, one mindset within Back to the Roots is that "I don't know" is never an acceptable answer. Between the internet and your social networks, all answers can be discovered in a short amount of time. Speed is simply a component of today's new normal.

Recently, the company secured a last-minute meeting with the number-one buyer at one of its national distribution partners. On the agenda for the meeting, which was scheduled to happen just three days later, was to share with the buyer what ideas they had in the "pipeline" about future products. This was a tremendous opportunity for the young company, and they didn't want to blow it. There was only one challenge: They didn't have any ideas in the pipeline.

But that didn't stop them. They dove into a "full-throttle R&D process" online to develop ideas for a new line of product extensions. Between their research and use of 3D modeling software, they were able to develop a fairly comprehensive presentation of several possible new products during the three-day lead-up to the meeting. The buyer was very impressed, prompting him to ask the owners "Why didn't you bring this to me earlier?" We're not sure they admitted to him that these fully researched and designed product prototypes didn't even exist three days earlier.

What Is Fast?

Back to the Roots has what every organization covets: speed. We have said it several times in this book, and you hear it almost daily in the business press: The pace of change has gone through the roof, and our organizations are not keeping up. A strategic window opens up, but the organization can't pivot fast enough and loses out to that creative new startup. The development of new technology being used both by our competitors and by our customers makes it almost impossible to stay ahead of the curve, and we find ourselves scrambling to keep up. Executives stay up at night worrying about speed, or the lack thereof.

Speed, of course, is a key variable in any calculation of productivity and efficiency. The cost of your widget factory won't change once it gets built, so the faster you can get widgets to roll off of the assembly line, the more productive and profitable you will be in a given period of time. If you run a call center and can shorten your average call time, you are able to handle a higher volume of calls with the same number of staff. Speed almost always translates into cost savings or increased profits. From many different perspectives, faster seems to be better.

Invest in Speed

Speed does come at a cost, however. We've all heard the warning from consultants and other service professionals: fast, good, or cheap—pick two. If you want things done very quickly (fast) and you want high quality (good), then you should expect to pay more for that (not cheap). Or, conversely, if you want it fast and cheap, that's fine, but you'd better lower the bar in terms of quality. Speed always requires tradeoffs.

But, in today's economy, it's not the clients' demand for speed at low cost and high quality that is forcing our hand; it is our competitors. In every market, the companies that invest in generating speed are the ones that get ahead, so, while speed may have a cost, smart companies consider it an investment that generates good returns. Manufacturing firms, for example, seek to reduce the tradeoffs between quality and speed by investing in quality-improvement programs like Six Sigma while also using new lean manufacturing principles that eliminate waste and increase speed. While we have increased productivity and efficiency tremendously over the last century, there is always room to improve, and that pushes us to look for ways to do things faster.

> We are not first to market when it comes to keeping up with new trends and demand for speed in today's business environment. Unless you can find someone through word of mouth or by connecting on our internal intranet, it is next to impossible to know what people are working on in a different department. We work in silos and struggle to understand how our business is keeping up—more so for me, as someone who has been in the company for a year. I can't see what we're doing to keep up. Every day, it feels like we are falling more and more behind.
> —*Millennial, b. 1991*

Small Steps and Big Leaps

Is that what was happening at Back to the Roots? Not entirely. There are two kinds of speed in the business world. First, there is the speed that you gain by making incremental improvements on existing processes. Lean processes focus on capturing this kind of speed, and, although it is incremental, it is still important. Incremental speed gains can account for major swings in market share in many industries, and, given that our current global economy is pushing our entire ecosystem to its limits, the combined impact of incremental efficiency gains is significant. We're going to need every single incremental speed improvement that we can find if we want to sustain ourselves.

The second kind of speed—exhibited by Back to the Roots—is more of a leap than an incremental step. It's the kind of speed that makes people stop, shake their heads, and say, "How did they do that?!" Based on the resources Back to the Roots had at its disposal and the rules of the game by which we presume everyone in that situation would be playing, it achieved a measure of speed (creating viable new product lines in only three days) that flat-out doesn't make sense. When Zappos went from $1 million in sales to $1 billion in sales in just eight years (two years ahead of its own schedule), we had a similar reaction. It just doesn't seem possible to grow that fast when your primary business already has an air of impossibility around it (such as selling shoes via the internet). General McChrystal's use of transparency to enable his people to jump from running 18 operations a month to more than 300 is the same kind of leap.

This second kind of speed is the focus of this chapter. **As a capacity that drives organizational success in today's world, incremental speed is important, but the kind of speed that enables you to leap ahead when the context demands it is in fact more critical.** This, of course, is precisely the kind of speed that has defined social media's growth. Media from previous eras, like television, could take their time growing. It took 13 years after the launch of television to reach a viewership of 50 million people. Facebook, on the other hand, has not yet hit its 13th birthday, but it has already amassed more than 1.2 billion active users. Even Google Plus managed to secure its first 25 million unique visitors in only two months (yes, months, not years) even though the market was already quite saturated with social networks at launch and its promise not well articulated. Today's social world moves fast.

> We are keeping up in the sense that we are acutely aware of the massive changes happening both in the general business environment and within the association and association-management spaces. We keep up with trends and have plenty of opportunities for continuing education both internally and externally. However, we are behind in that we have not fully transitioned from a 20th-century company (doing things the way they've always been done) to one that is nimble, flexible, and fast to respond to market changes.
>
> —*Millennial, b. 1983*

Why Millennials Care About Fast

The speed of today's social internet is just fine for the Millennials. It's all they have ever known. While the rest of us may be amazed that the smartphones we hold in our hands have more computing power than the computers our astronauts used to land on the moon (actually, even the early PCs in the 1980s were significantly more powerful than the ones we had earlier used for space travel), Millennials can get frustrated if it takes more than 12 months for the new version of the iPhone to be released. That's not because they are an "entitled" generation; it's because for many years Apple did release a new phone once a year (in addition to developing multiple editions of other products like computers, iPads, etc.). **What seems fast to the rest of us is normal to Millennials.**

And when they show up in the workplace, these differing standards become more obvious. The Millennials we consulted in our research seemed almost confused by their organizations' inability to quickly shift and adapt to a new reality. This wasn't unanimous—plenty of the Millennials we spoke to felt their organizations were doing a good job keeping up with the times—but there were many who could not understand why their organizations (and particularly the senior leaders) were still so committed to doing things the way they had always been done. As one Millennial said:

> They are not keeping up with the speed. They are very stuck in their ways and promote the individuals who want to keep it slow. New, young workers come in with great ideas and fresh perspectives, but the older folks just keep it the "way that it is" and resist trying new things.

The result is a drag on innovation, which also seems to be connected to issues of organizational structure and hierarchy. The senior staff tend to be the ones who are clinging to the way things have always been done, but, even if they weren't, the process of getting the requisite sign-offs from senior staff slows things down in ways that frustrate Millennials.

116

There seems to be a subtle attitude of "this is how we've always done things" that, at times, can stifle innovation or self-evaluation. This isn't an issue that's limited just to our office but rather seems to be a symptom of the entire organization's structure. … Sometimes the flow of information up and down the leadership structure can quickly bog down leading to delays in making decisions. Typically this is just due to busy schedules and isn't intentional, but when each decision needs multiple sign-offs and a meeting scheduled, it can take weeks.

Remember that one of the key societal trends that has shaped the Millennial generation was abundance, and the continuous release of new iPhones is just one example. Since they were children, they have been dealt a continuous stream of not just new tools but game-changing technology. Older generations get frustrated when they invest time and energy learning and setting up systems to support the use of a particular piece of technology or software, only to have it become obsolete within a short period of time, but Millennials simply drop it and move on to the next thing. **Millennials let go easily, while the rest of us hold on, and that's an important lesson for all of us.**

What Fast Looks Like

Letting go is at the heart of what it means to be fast. More specifically, it is the letting go of control. You don't have to let go of control to make incremental improvements in speed. In that scenario, the basic boundaries of the system are not challenged; you simply maximize efficiency within a set of well-understood norms. But, to achieve the speed that enables a leap to the next level, you have to push past those boundaries, and that requires you to let go of control. As car racing great Mario Andretti once said:

If everything seems under control, you're just not going fast enough.

Back to the Roots relied on the power of the internet and the most current software to develop its proposal for new product lines, and that enabled its team to complete the task in a matter of days. Other companies might not have been willing to move that quickly. They might have needed time to develop and test prototypes before making the pitch. They might have needed experts to sign off first. Those activities are put in place to keep things more under their control. Giving up that kind of control would feel too risky, thus they never achieve the speed that Back to the Roots did.

Giving up control, of course, is not an easy thing to do, particularly as a leader in an organization. People are counting on you, and there's a lot on the line if mistakes are made. That's why we establish controls in the first place. So, to enable speed, we can't just flatly demand that leaders give up control, because they won't. What we need to do is offer them something in return for giving up control:

Trust.

Human beings will give up control (and thus expose themselves to risk) when they have someone or something in which they can place their trust. You give all of your money over to the bank because you trust that it has competent people and the right processes in place to keep it safe. It's a risk you are willing to take because you have trust in the system, and you're able to move around a lot faster not dragging those suitcases of cash with you. **Trust lets you give up control, and that makes things faster.**

> I think our organization is trying to take the steps to keep up with the rapid pace of change and increased demand for speed in today's business environment. I think that our organization is having a hard time with upper staff, who have been with the company for 10+ years, who don't have the fast work ethic that the younger generation has. It is hard for the organization to address this without changing the roles of the loyal staff. I think the organization is attempting to integrate the Millennial generation into upper management.
>
> —*Millennial, b. 1989*

In his book *The Speed of Trust*, Stephen M.R. Covey tells the story of how Warren Buffett of Berkshire Hathaway was able to conclude a $23 billion acquisition of Walmart's transportation division in approximately one month, initially over a handshake, primarily because he trusted the operation to be just as Walmart said it would be. Southwest Airlines CEO Herb Kelleher reportedly approved the reorganization of the airline's $700 million maintenance organization based on the review of a three-page memo and a single question to the leader of that division.[56] When you trust people, you are able to move more quickly. Trust enables speed.

For an entire organization to become fast, however, it goes beyond trusting the competence of the people you work with (though that's certainly a good start). A fast organization will build an entire system of trust to achieve the kind of speed that enables them to leap to new levels, rather than settle for incremental improvements. A system of trust is built around a keystone—that one stone in an arch that keeps the other stones from falling to the ground. The keystone in a trust system is a core concept that is the primary source of trust that allows the release of control.

For Back to the Roots, the keystone was the power of the internet and the skill of its staff in accessing that power. Knowing that everyone there could tap into the internet's immense power meant they didn't have to spend as much time verifying or testing possibilities. It's not that they didn't verify or test at all—trust is not designed to release all control, just some of it—but they did less of it than would traditionally be deemed necessary, and that unlocked the speed.

That worked for Back to the Roots, but it does not necessarily make it a model for everyone. Many different keystones can be used to create a system of trust in an organization that will make it faster.

I would build more lateral teams based on mutual work and trust and create more opportunity to get to know people personally. I would create seating arrangements based on either teams, personalities, strengths, and the like. I would also have a lot of transparency, not just from upper management but also middle management.

—*Millennial, b. 1984*

Case Study: Happy State Bank

Consider the example of Happy State Bank, a community bank in Texas. The bank was founded in Happy, a small town in the Texas panhandle, just south of Amarillo. Happy has a population of less than 1,000 people, and if you are not from the area but have actually heard of Happy, Texas, it is probably because you either drove past it (it's hard to forget the sign that declares it to be "the town without a frown") or you've seen the 1999 film by that name (a comedy about two escaped convicts hiding out in Happy, although it wasn't even filmed there).

Like any community bank, Happy State Bank started small. Twenty-five years ago, it was a $10 million bank, with only six employees, ranked 812th out of approximately 880 banks in Texas. Today, its rank is up to 25th, and it turned that $10 million into $2.5 billion, now with 33 offices stretching out as far as Dallas.

A key factor in the bank's growth has been its capacity for speed. CEO J. Pat Hickman likes to tell the story of a friend of his who managed the branch of a bank in Plainview, Texas, just outside of Lubbock. That bank was in the process of being acquired by a company headquartered in Spain, and the branch manager was not thrilled at the prospect of working for a much larger bank, so he reached out to Pat, whom he knew, trusted, and thought might be interested in opening a branch in Plainview. Pat went to Plainview that day, they met with key customers, and just four days later they had remodeled a local bike shop into the newest branch of Happy State Bank, open and ready for business. (It turns out they have a room at headquarters filled with the necessary supplies and equipment for what they call "branch startup kits," so when such opportunities arise, they can react quickly.)

The bank is also well known for processing business loans much more quickly than many of its competitors. Local loan committees are given authority to approve loans at a higher level than other banks. While other banks would need to send an application through to headquarters in New York to get approval on a $30,000 loan, local Happy State Bank loan committees make much larger loans without needing central approval. "Our local committees don't have to wait," said Senior Banking Officer Gary Wells. "If you have an immediate need, we'll react quickly. A quick no is better than a long maybe or a long no."

They really, truly care about their people

Given the recent crises in the financial industry that played a significant role in one of the most extensive economic downturns in our history, Happy State Bank's process of turning over control to its local committees might seem like a bad idea, but the system is not about recklessness or even increased risk. Its leaders know full well that banks go under because of bad loans and that asset quality is of primary importance, and its loan committees are making good decisions. At the time that we interviewed employees as part of our research, Wells noted that only 20 out of the bank's roughly 12,000 loans were 30 days or more past due. The only reason it can release control to the local committees is because it has built a system in which those local committees end up making better decisions. **Interestingly, Happy State Bank's system is based on the disciplined and rigorous focus on two things that are not typically associated with the world of banking and finance: caring and relationships.**

> I want my employees to love where they work. I also want them to feel as if they are working in an environment with people who genuinely care about their well-being. That will help with recruitment and retention.
>
> —*Millennial, b. 1984*

Everyone we talked to at Happy State Bank cares deeply about both customers and fellow employees. While lines of authority are clear, that never gets in the way of building a strong relationship with a coworker. They say things like "he works with me, not for me," and new hires at the lower levels are often amazed to find that the most senior people in the bank take the time to get to know them and always make themselves accessible. According to Bank Officer Rian Clinton:

> *When an employee asks me to do something, I do it because I care about them. It's genuine. It's not made up.*

They all contribute to a fund that is used to help out employees who hit a rough spot or incur unexpected expenses. They set up a prayer request list on their intranet where employees can ask each other for prayers. The bank supports employees in moving into different positions based on their career growth. "We want employees to succeed," said Bank Officer Sean Workman, "so we do what we can."

This level of care extends to their customers as well. Happy State Bank is not the only company to focus on customer service, of course, but its focus seems to emanate from that same basic, human level of caring that they have for their coworkers. Despite the bank's growth over the years, it has never opened a call center—it wants customers to call the employees at their bank. It's personal, and the bank's leaders expect employees to know their customers at a deep level and genuinely care about them. As we mentioned in Chapter 3, Happy State Bank employees have been known to actually travel to customers' homes to help them log into the online banking system. They care deeply, and they show it.

They build real relationships internally and externally

All this caring has a point: building relationships. Strong relationships, both with customers and among employees, is the keystone to Happy State Bank's system of trust, and that enables the speed. When Bank Officer Lisa Kirkwood moved to Iowa for three years and left her job (temporarily) at Happy State Bank, she said she mourned leaving her bank family as much as her real family. The internal relationships were that strong.

The first point in the Happy State Bank Credo is about the relationship with the customer.

I will treat customers with the same courtesy and respect I would expect if I were in their position. Every contact is an opportunity to establish or to strengthen a relationship.

Again, it may sound like straight-up customer service, but the relationships enable speed. As they build strong relationships with customers (based on truly caring for them), then the customers end up sharing more information with the bank. They will tell the bank why they are making a request or what they have been struggling with related to that request. Most companies have to poll their customers to get information from them, but Happy State Bank customers proactively share information, and that enables the bank employees to be more proactive and nimble in meeting their needs. When the bank staff know the customers and their communities so well, they will be able to see when key information is missing on a loan application and tell them up front, rather than waiting for that application to be returned from the processing center in New York requesting more information.

Internal relationships enable speed as well. The strong relationships across layers of the hierarchy enable a greater flow of ideas and innovation. When you have direct access to senior bank officials, including the CEO (who not only knows your name but has a reputation for never having mispronounced any employee's name), then you'll share more ideas internally. According to bank employee Sabrina Shields, this enables the whole system to lose some of its fear about new ideas from all levels, and "that's where greatness comes from; you don't want to hold greatness down."

When local loan committees do hit their upper limit and need approval from headquarters, the senior staff have already invested in deep relationships with all of their employees. They know the local loan committees so well that they can easily trust their assessments and can quickly find the issues that need greater scrutiny.

It may sound touchy-feely, but the investment in relationships pays off in terms of speed. Strong relationships create the trust needed to let go of control just enough to maintain extraordinary speed without increasing risk unnecessarily.

Takeaways: Make Your Organization Fast

Remember that true organizational speed is a deep capacity, not just a momentary focus on moving more quickly. A world-class sprinter doesn't just decide to run fast—she spends years training and building the capacity to achieve that kind of speed. So, be prepared to work on speed at several different levels.

Start With the Low-Hanging Fruit

To reach the second level of fast that we have been talking about in this chapter, which Back to the Roots does through its trust in the internet and Happy State Bank does through its trust in its community, it typically helps to have achieved the first level of fast to begin with. Fast organizations are disciplined about achieving efficiency and productivity that keeps them at the top of their field. This is a good first step because it starts with understanding your business inside and out. You have to know how things work to be able to maximize efficiency and productivity. This is actually in line with Millennial sensibilities. Millennials grew up with unparalleled abundance, and as a result come to the workplace with high standards. They expect simple problems to already have been solved, and that includes basic efficiency and productivity. They grew up in a very fast world and as a generation seem to be frustrated with the slow speeds of organizations. Ari Lightman, a professor at Carnegie Mellon, shared with us that his graduate students are used to collaborating on multiple projects, using their networks, but then suddenly they are thrust into the world of professional work where everything moves at a snail's pace. Smart organizations will invest in understanding their own businesses deeply in order to maximize their basic levels of speed to help keep Millennials engaged.

> Teleworking, utilizing Lync, flexible schedules—people produce their best work at various times and I believe allowing employees to work in environments that are conducive to that is important. It takes a team to really produce quality work fast, so ensuring all staff are receiving the necessary professional development opportunities is also another way to ensure they are keeping up with the demand for speed.
>
> —*Millennial, b. 1984*

Figure Out Digital, Clear, and Fluid

Reviewing the previous three chapters in this book can help as well. The other three capacities that we have identified—Digital, Clear, and Fluid— all contribute to increased speed.

Invest in technology and build a digital mindset

One of the points of using digital technology has always been to help get the job done faster. Many organizations would do well just to review exactly how they use their existing technology and update their practices to reflect the current reality of the marketplace. In other words, let's stop using email as an instant messaging tool, and just because the senior managers like SharePoint doesn't mean it has to be the answer for every project management problem. Take a look at how you can embrace the digital mindset (disciplined focus on the user or customer), because that too can generate speed—just look at Happy State Bank.

Get information where it needs to go

Clarity also enables speed, as evidenced by General McChrystal's results in Iraq. As he stated, information is only valuable when it is in the hands of people who can use that information to make things better. When you use transparency to get more information in the hands of more people, you inevitably increase your speed. As we suggest in Chapter 4, take a hard look at your decision-making processes to see where transparency can be inserted, because that will help those processes move more swiftly. We also suggest taking a look internally at who has access to whom. Happy State Bank has demonstrated the importance of that kind of broad access in enabling its speed.

Give power to those on the ground

Flattening the hierarchy has long been held up as a way to battle the lethargic nature of bureaucracy. If the first step to becoming faster in an organization is understanding your business inside and out to maximize efficiency in productivity, then the next step is to apply that knowledge, as we suggested in Chapter 5, to understanding what truly drives success, because that is at the heart of activating a flatter and more fluid hierarchy. Then you can move onto investing in soft skills like conflict resolution, because when people can work through conflict easily, everything can get done faster.

This is why fast is the last of the four capacities we explore in this book. While the other three are not prerequisites for becoming a fast organization, the work you go through to achieve those other three capacities will set you up nicely for succeeding in being fast as well.

Find the Key to Unlocking Speed

Once you have set the stage for speed by mastering efficiency and productivity, the next step is to identify and develop the unique keystone that holds together the trust system that will unlock that next level of speed for your organization. This will not be easy work. Remember, the purpose of creating a system of trust is to enable you to give up some control. It is only when you can let go of control that you can truly achieve leap-forward speed.

Define what drives the success of the enterprise

Of course, it's not about just letting go of control in general. You want the speed that gets results, that sets you apart, that amazes your customers, and leaves behind your competition. That means the areas of control you relinquish must be directly tied to unlocking greater potential in the system. In other words, identifying the keystone in your trust system starts with a deep clarity of what drives the success of your organization to begin with.

As we discussed at the end of the previous chapter, determining what drives your organization's success requires going one level beyond what is strategically obvious. For QLI, that means going beyond providing excellent healthcare to injured patients and focusing more carefully on what it means to actually rebuild shattered lives. **You will need to figure out what that strategic clarity is for your organization and then build in to your processes, systems, and structures the necessary elements to deliver on that promise.** All the organizations we've profiled in this book have done that well.

> Overall, we are far more resilient to competitiveness issues and attrition than most because we don't wait for the market to make the issue apparent. We are proactive, though not overzealous in enacting too many initiatives at once.
>
> —*Millennial, b. 1987*

Use blue ocean thinking to identify the keystone

Strategic clarity by itself does not give you the keystone for your trust system, however. As you work to figure out where you can let go of control in order to get the leap-forward kind of speed that we're talking about, we encourage you to do some "blue ocean" thinking.

That term comes from W. Chan Kim and Renée Mauborgne's classic strategy text from 2005 titled *Blue Ocean Strategy*.[57] Their research explored companies that had managed to redefine the core elements of their business model in ways that left them in a market space virtually free of competition (a blue ocean, as opposed to the "bloody red ocean" of competition). Southwest Airlines was a prime example. Instead of competing against the other airlines along all of the same dimensions of a traditional airline business model, Southwest completely eliminated some traditional aspects of air travel (first class cabins and airport lounges), shifted emphasis to others (quick turnaround times), and then added some new elements (staff that could be themselves and have fun on the job). In the end, Southwest didn't attempt to beat the other airlines at their own game. It redefined the game instead, to its own advantage of course. That is the essence of blue ocean thinking applied in the context of strategy: you raise, create, reduce, or eliminate key aspects of the strategy formula on which the competitors in your industry rely, and that gives you the exclusive access to the expansive the blue oceans.

This approach can be modified to help you find the keystone for your trust system. In this case, instead of focusing on strategic elements and how you compete externally, you find your keystone by analyzing the internal leadership practices that define your culture. Look at the senior management level, for example. Maybe your senior management has a bad habit of demanding an onerous amount of detailed reporting from lower levels, which slows down the organization by preventing people from taking action on pressing issues when they need to. Or maybe your senior management tends to pass the buck when they get negative feedback from customers or members, which results in lower levels of trust from the customers or members, who feel like their concerns are being ignored. On the positive side, let's say your senior management excels at establishing and communicating a clear vision, which helps people at other levels row in the same direction, so to speak.

To use blue ocean thinking, you would make a complete list of all the critical habits and approaches of your senior management, and then apply the four lenses of raise, reduce, create, and eliminate to set your organization apart. Maybe you would strive to eliminate time senior management spent reviewing detailed reports, or perhaps you could find ways to expand their efforts in communicating a clear vision. By eliminating, increasing, creating, and reducing, you would be doing what Kim and Mauborgne call repainting your "leadership canvas," and the changes you make give you access to blue ocean leadership.[58]

To bring your keystone into the picture, you simply **focus on elements of your leadership canvas that relate to increasing trust and letting go of control, since that is what enables speed.** Getting rid of those reports, being clearer on the vision, and responding directly to customers would be priorities for you, because not only are they good ideas for leadership but they all focus on increasing trust, reducing control, and increasing speed. Of course, those are just elements you identified by examining your senior management level. A full analysis would include middle managers and line supervisors, as well. When you can identify the key elements from all of these levels, you will likely be able to discover that unique keystone that will unlock that leap-to-the-next-level kind of speed. For Happy State Bank, its detailed analysis of the leadership needs at every level of management ended up pointing to the keystone of strong relationships. For Back to the Roots, it was trusting in the internet, cutting-edge software, and a staff that isn't afraid to use those tools. Once you find yours, you'll be able to make the necessary changes to your culture and start accessing the speed.

From Fast to Digital

We encouraged you above to go back to the other three chapters: Digital, Clear, and Fluid. Why? Because if we are really to embrace these principles, which are fundamentally about turning our rigid, mechanical systems into human-powered, evolutionary ecosystems, then that means the work is never done. We need to keep iterating (and leaping). We need to keep examining our mindsets and checking that our structures haven't already become as outdated as our clunky database software. We need to keep defining the values that drive our success, because those aren't static either. That idea may exhaust you, or, if you're like many Millennials, it may exhilarate you. Either way, change is happening and it's not slowing down. Instead of fearing it, embrace optimism around the possibilities that change unlocks for your organization.

If you feel in control, then you're not going fast enough. Feel the wind in your hair and let go just enough to let the exhilaration flow. We are talking about a revolution in management, after all.

Now is not the time to hesitate.

;)

7. Proceed Until Apprehended

The revolution is coming.

It has before, of course, and it will again. The particular revolution we have written about in this book involves leadership, management, and business, but, as we pointed out in Chapter 2, this four-season cycle has been happening at a generational level for centuries. We pulled through the Great Depression and World War II. We survived the Civil War. We emerged victorious after our struggle for independence in the Revolutionary War. Every four generations we have faced a dark and cold winter, and each time, spring eventually arrived. The same is true today. Spring is coming.

And each time, there was a generation entering adulthood that led the charge. They did not do it alone, but they were in a life stage that put them in the position of leading, and they stepped up to the challenge. Today they are the Millennials. For those of us who have been around the block (i.e., Generation Xers and Baby Boomers), all this attention on the Millennials might be off-putting, but remember that everyone plays a role on a heroic journey. For every Luke Skywalker (Millennial), there is always a need for an Obi-Wan Kenobi (Baby Boomer), and even an occasional cynical and independent Han Solo (Generation Xer). We know it is cliché, but we're all in this together.

Togetherness turns out to be a key concept when it comes to these major generational shifts. For each of the previous "fourth turnings," togetherness and unity were central to our success in making the transition. Think of the "join or die" flags from the American Revolution or simply preserving the Union in the Civil War. Even the end of the Depression and World War II were about coming together in community to both rebuild the economy and prevent the spread of dictatorship in the world. **To get through the hard times, we come together. Like optimism, this is a key component of successful revolution.** As we work through those hard times, we must relearn how to be in community with each other. All of this coming together is not about mere collaboration—it is about intentionally building and nurturing community.

Community

You might be thinking, what does "community" have to do with the future of business?

Let's take a closer look at the four organizations we profiled in the previous four chapters and see how the ideas of community and togetherness are woven into the capacities of Digital, Clear, Fluid, and Fast.

The American Society for Surgery of the Hand showed us how to be digital. ASSH has not hesitated to invest in digital technology, and, more importantly, it fully embraces the digital mindset, designing its offerings with the customer in mind and designing the organization around the experience of the employees. As a result, productivity has increased. When the culture is designed around the needs of the employees, they get more done. It also increases engagement. "This place cares more about us, so we should care more about this place," as one employee put it. They are agile and adaptable—the employee-centered workplace makes it easier for different people to jump in and help with different tasks throughout the year. They are proactive. They innovate. And they do it all together—literally, as all their desks are together in one room. Staff meetings are staff-led rather than leader-led every other week. They value the power of their community.

Menlo Innovations is actually in the digital industry, but it showed us how to be clear. Its programmers work in pairs so code is actually made visible as it is being written, and its project management system is literally taped to the wall for everyone to see. The Menlo staff even show all of this to their customers, who come to the office to help with the planning. All of this transparency enables everyone in the system to make smarter decisions. The code is higher quality, the users' needs are better reflected in the final product, and internal problems and challenges are solved directly, without needing managers. And Menlo, too, cares about community. Like ASSH, the staff all work together in one big room, and they start every day with a quick, 15-minute, stand-up all-staff meeting where each pair talks about what they are working on. They even end the meeting with a reference to the Hill Street Blues television show, telling everyone to "be careful out there." They won't hesitate to support new parents bringing in babies to work (rather than having the parents work from home), because they value working together as a group. Yes, the CEO has been on the phone with an important client while holding a noisy baby, because that's how you support each other in a community. Community matters.

QLI is a healthcare company that showed us what it means to be fluid. It has a hierarchy, but it is flexible, and decisions get made based on who has the relevant knowledge about the patient—not just medically but also in the context of the patient's hopes and dreams. This allows QLI staff to accomplish amazing things and solve the stickiest problems (they are rebuilding shattered lives, after all) while sparking true ownership behavior at every level. And they recognize that they can only maintain these results with a strong internal community. They invest in soft skills like conflict resolution to help people strengthen relationships. They even have a set of internal roles (called mentors and professionals) that is outside of the traditional hierarchy and designed specifically to support and nurture their culture to make sure their community stays strong.

And, finally, Happy State Bank, even though it is in a strongly regulated industry, showed us how to be fast. Leveraging the power of both internal and external relationships, it has built a system of trust that allows its staff to let go of just enough control so they can leap ahead of competitors. Deeper relationships reveal problems sooner and speed up the solutions, as well, resulting in rapid growth that never requires them to give up their culture of caring. Family and community have remained at the heart of the bank's culture and its success.

When we pulled these four capacities out of our research, we were focused on the important ways that they address the concrete and pervasive business problems organizations face in today's economy, and the case study organizations demonstrated this power clearly. By choosing to be digital, clear, fluid, and fast, they achieve greater productivity and more frequent innovation. They are able to solve problems more quickly and thoroughly, and they are more adept at creating solutions that work for their customers. They are not only beating their competition soundly; they do it while solving two of the most vexing management problems that the traditional machine approach has given us: dire employee engagement and lack of organizational agility.

We wrote this book as a practical guide, showing leaders tangible practices that could improve results and enable a greater impact. Digital, Clear, Fluid, and Fast will do that for you. But along the way, we noticed another layer to the insights from the research. Innovation, productivity, agility, and problem solving seemed to be accompanied by a different set of organizational results that reflected the "softer side" of business: things like engagement, relationships, caring, culture, family, trust, joy, and, of course, community. You can see this in each of the case study organizations. **Digital, Clear, Fluid, and Fast, while objectively powerful by themselves, will be more successful when they are connected to the capacities needed for strong community.**

Remember what we said in Chapter 2: The most effective solutions in the future of business will be connected to today's unique historical context, and today's context is a fourth turning, a transition from winter to spring, where coming together in community matters. Some of the ideas that we present in this book are not particularly new, but, when they were introduced as alternatives to traditional management in the past, they were never fully adopted because the historical context was not right for it.

In the 1920s, for example, Harvard Business School professor Elton Mayo conducted a series of experiments at the Hawthorne plant of the Western Electric Company outside of Chicago that focused specifically on the human aspect of doing work. The researchers originally set out to determine the optimal light level for doing work at the plant, but they accidentally discovered an even more important principle: When you show that you actually care about the workers by asking them which lighting level they prefer, you increase their performance—regardless of which lighting scheme you choose. (This principle became known as the "Hawthorne effect.")[59] Now, nearly 100 years later, we are highlighting the work of Happy State Bank and how deeply its leaders care about both their customers and their employees, and the reason why this idea will stick today, when it failed to during the last century, is that **our transition today needs human community to work, when the transition last century needed machines.**

If you want to leap ahead of your competition, and if you want to successfully ride the waves of this perfect storm that will come to a head in the next several years, then you need to integrate the four capacities we have discussed with the human and community-focused aspects of business at the same time. You may by now have recognized that this is what most of the darlings of the business press have been doing for the last several years (e.g., Zappos, Whole Foods, Google, Morning Star, Netflix, and others). We read so many glowing stories about these companies all over the internet these days, not just because these companies are doing things differently but because they are supremely successful in making a profit at the same time.

If you build up your capacity for Digital, Clear, Fluid, and Fast and make sure they are integrated with trust, caring, relationships, and a strong community, you can do this too. The reason Millennials are champions for these ideas—not just in general, but specifically to help you, inside your company—is that these principles come naturally to them for reasons we've explained. We all need to work together to batten down our hatches; the perfect storm hasn't hit in full force yet. The capacities of Digital, Clear, Fluid, and Fast are not as prevalent as they need to be. We need to start now.

We gave you concrete takeaways in each of the previous four chapters, places you can start making preparations and changes, by:

- Innovating your HR practice
- Reviewing your decision-making processes
- Designing a transparency architecture
- Investing in soft skills
- Finding the keystone of your trust system.

We gave you a lot of actionable ideas in this book, but as you look at the list of things to work on, you will notice that most of them are embedded in an area that we have talked about frequently in this book but haven't focused on fully: culture.

Culture

We have all seen organizational culture rising in importance in the business world over the last few years. "Culture" is, as a matter of fact, Merriam-Webster's Word of the Year for 2014.[60] Some have already claimed that ideas like culture and employee engagement have already become too popular and graduated to the level of buzzwords.

We don't think so.

The rapidly rising attention these ideas are getting is not because they have become the fad of the day; rather, it is because culture is particularly relevant to management's transition from the industrial world to the digital age. It is because the future of business is inextricably linked to community, and you can't build community without a strong and (more importantly) intentional culture. **That is one thing that every one of our case study organizations had in common to begin with: They have strong and powerful cultures that allow them to attract both the best customers and the best employees**. And none of these cultures is an accident.

Yet most cultures are accidental. We tend to put nearly all of our attention on running the business and only think about culture during the occasional offsite retreat where we wordsmith a list of core values. Culture needs more than a list of values posted on the wall. (For the record, Enron had a nice set of values posted in its lobby, too.) Remember the definition of culture that we shared in Chapter 4:

Organizational culture is the collection of words, actions, thoughts, and "stuff" that clarifies and reinforces what a company truly values.

The words you put on the wall are a part of it, but culture is also defined by everyone's actions, the underlying thought processes and assumptions, and the tangible parts of how your organization works (office layout, office location, technology used, etc.) that make it crystal clear to everyone exactly what is valued internally. It's less about the lofty values and more about clarity on what is truly valued on a day-to-day basis.

At Menlo Innovations, employees deeply value collaboration and transparency, and they make that clear in a number of different ways, perhaps the most obvious being their process of having two programmers share one computer as they write their code. (Collaboration is not optional when you share a mouse and a keyboard.) But just dictating collaboration is never enough; you need to make a clear connection between what is valued and why that drives success inside the organization.

We sat in on a performance feedback meeting at Menlo that one of the developers there (let's call him John) had organized. There is no annual process at Menlo where the boss makes you fill out a form; when you want feedback to help you grow and improve, you convene a meeting of your peers over lunch and you discuss your progress. A key part of this particular conversation during John's feedback meeting was about a direction he took on a particular project without making it visible to the rest of the team. He experimented with some new code, but off to the side, knowing there had been resistance to the suggestion before. Eventually he realized that doing this work "in secret" went against their company culture. Whether or not it was good code, it wasn't how code is written at Menlo, so he deleted it. One of his colleagues in the review meeting thanked him, and then went further to explain why that was so important. Their code is written collaboratively and visibly so that the entire team can "play the chess moves out seven or eight moves ahead" as the code is developing. Writing something off to the side robs the team of that ability, to the detriment of the final result. In other words, transparency and collaboration leads to better software in their particular context. It drives success. That is cultural clarity. And that was not accidental. CEO Rich Sheridan and his business partner James Goebel created Menlo Innovations with this culture specifically in mind (and they created it in 2001, at the depths of the software world's depression, but succeeded from the get-go).

Which brings us back to you. You are not Rich Sheridan. You may not even be the CEO, and even if you are, you are probably not in the position to start an organization from scratch like Rich did. You already work for an organization, and that organization already has a culture. If you are lucky, the culture is an intentional one, but it is more likely that the culture is at least partly accidental. It evolved and morphed over the years, primarily in response to what the people in the organization thought the CEO wanted.

Founder Culture

Your task is to turn that around. Obviously we believe you should make your organization more digital, clear, fluid, and fast, but as you work on that you need to also ensure that these ideas are woven into the fabric of your culture, rather than being implemented as the cool new processes you read about in a business book. You need to make that additional shift, from an accidental culture to an intentional one.

If you are the CEO, then it quite literally means making culture your job. It is probably already somewhere in your job description, but most CEOs put that in the category of "Yes I'm in charge of that, because the buck stops here, but it doesn't occupy too much of my attention." That is a sure-fire path to an accidental culture. **CEOs must actively choose their culture, or it will be chosen for them.** And doing that one offsite meeting where you come up with the generic core values (honesty, integrity, excellence, etc.) so you can check the box on culture is not enough. Employees can smell a partial commitment to culture a mile away, and it won't stick. Instead, they will look past the bland values statement and scrutinize your actual statements and your actual behavior and then invent a culture based on that. We are not sure why employees routinely cede that power to shape culture to the CEO, but they do.

That is why you must make culture your job. We know you have tons of other things to do, but you might want to find ways to delegate some of that (which might be easier if your organization were fluid—hint, hint), because a strong culture must be lived and breathed by the CEO. It needs to be top of mind and practiced consistently, and it needs your nurturing and attention. Employees need to see consistency between what you say the culture is and how you practice it, or they will go back to deciding on their own what the culture is. All the CEOs of the organizations we profiled took culture this seriously, and you've seen the results they've achieved. Do the work of understanding your current culture (see the Takeaways in Chapter 4), connect that to what drives the success of your organization (see the Takeaways in Chapter 5), and make it your job to create a strong culture that attracts.

Grassroots Culture

If you are not the CEO, you are still not off the hook. Just because employees cede the power to define an organization's culture to the CEO does not mean they have to; **you have the power to shape things from your**

position regardless of where you sit. As much as the CEO has the power to define an organization's culture, the fact remains that the culture is brought to life through all the employees. Good CEOs get this, of course, and their actions are actually designed to nurture the cultural norms among employees so they behave in those ways naturally. So, making culture your job is partly about simply living the culture intentionally. If those value statements that hang on the wall actually help you to be more successful in your work, then pay attention to both your behaviors and those of others and hold everyone accountable to those values. Be nice about it, but have the courage to call people out when they behave in ways that are inconsistent with the culture. If you don't, then the culture slips back into accidental mode. No one said having a strong culture would be easy.

It is possible, of course, that you will find yourself in an organization where the higher-ups don't see things the way you do. They might not yet value the potential that could be realized by becoming digital, clear, fluid, or fast. Whether it is accidental or intentional, they may have created an organization with a culture that you feel is not going to be compatible with the future of business. What do you do then? You start with a choice to stay or go. They say that people don't leave organizations; they leave managers. But, more frequently, it is the culture they are leaving, and the managers are simply reflecting that culture. **This big choice comes first, because life is short and you should love where you work.** So many people waste so much time and so much productivity because they defer that choice about staying or leaving based on either a fear of the unknown or a vague hope that their current situation will somehow get better. This is one reason why our engagement numbers are so low. Make your choice. Be bold. If it's not going to work where you are, then find (or create) a place where it will.

Starting with the choice also has a strong impact if you choose to stay in the organization, even if the culture is not the way you think it should be. **By choosing to stay, you plant a flag in the ground.** You choose to stay and choose to make things better.

So, get to it. Find the specific elements in this book that you think will have the biggest impact on organizational effectiveness and then design experiments to implement them. Since you are going against the existing culture, you should expect to encounter resistance, but in cases like these we always refer people to the mantra of Florence Nightingale as she went about the business of inventing the modern hospital: proceed until apprehended.

Proceed Until Apprehended

Don't wait for permission. Run as many experiments as you can. At some point you will be "apprehended" by someone who states that your approach is "not how we do things here" or questions why you are not using the standard process. When apprehended, you have an obligation to respond and explain why you are experimenting. It's never wise to just run over people who oppose you, but not having permission should not stop you.

If you really want to handle these "apprehensions" well, then make sure that you can articulate the positive results of all your previous experiments. Bosses love results. Too often, we try to convince them with the abstract reasons and thought processes behind a new approach, but because bosses already feel they have been getting adequate results from the current processes, those arguments always seem pale. When you can show them the results you got from the new way, though, they are more apt to listen.

Think back to Morning Star and that seasonal employee who bought a computer to enable data analysis at a specific point in his tomato processing. In that culture, he already had permission to buy that computer and run that experiment, but what if he didn't? Someone might have been angered when they saw the $1,500 charge on the corporate credit card, but when he could then explain how adding that computer saved the company X amount of dollars in the process, the transgression of existing culture and process would not seem so bad.

When you can introduce new processes and make the connection to results, then you are one step closer to making a shift in culture. There is still more work to be done to make it a culture shift, and much of that may be out of your control or your domain, but you still need to do your part. Stay focused on what works, measure results, and engage with the opposition. The worst that will happen is you get more evidence that your long-term future may not be with this company.

The Future of Business

It is an accident of history that you are reading this book right now, at a time when management has completed a four-season cycle and is on the edge of a new era. We could try to make a big deal out of that, even glorifying this moment, in an attempt to inspire you to take action. But glory is not the point. The point right now is focused, hard work, as it is in every major transition. We all need to put glory and individual accolades and gains on the back seat for a while, actually, and roll up our sleeves and work together to create the future of business.

The Millennial generation (again, by accident of history) holds a unique position in this process, not as the ones who will define or control this transition but as the ones who will most naturally understand what needs to be done. If you are a Millennial, then lend your voice to that cause. Push through the negative stereotypes like "entitled" and start building cultures that are digital, clear, fluid, and fast. If you are a Boomer or an Xer, look for opportunities to partner with Millennials in defining a new culture that is compatible with the forces that are coming together in the perfect storm that is transforming management. We all need to come together and create this next era, and that requires courage, conviction, clarity, and, above all, action. Each of us will follow a unique path, but we know one piece of advice that applies to everyone:

Proceed until apprehended.

Notes

1. Abby Ellin, "The Beat (Up) Generation," *Psychology Today,* March 11, 2014, http://www.psychologytoday.com/articles/201402/ the-beat-generation (accessed December 24, 2014).

2. Jamie Notter and Maddie Grant, *Humanize: How People-Centric Organizations Succeed in a Social World* (Indianapolis: Que Publishing, 2012).

3. Brigid Schulte, "New Poll: Reality May Bite, but 30-Somethings Stay Wildly Optimistic," *Washington Post,* October 9, 2014, http:// www.washingtonpost.com/news/local/wp/2014/10/09/new-poll-reality-may-bite-but-30-somethings-stay-wildly-optimistic/ (accessed December 20, 2014).

4. William Strauss and Neil Howe, *Generations: The History of America's Future, 1584 to 2069* (New York: Quill 1991).

5. William Strauss and Neil Howe, *The Fourth Turning: An American Prophecy—What the Cycles of History Tell Us About America's Next Rendezvous with Destiny* (New York: Broadway Books, 1997).

6. R. H. Franke and J. D. Kaul, "The Hawthorne experiments: First statistical interpretation," *American Sociological Review* 43 (1978): 623-643 (summarized at http://www.nwlink. com/~donclark/hrd/history/hawthorne.html, accessed December 20, 2014).

7. Douglas McGregor, *The Human Side of Enterprise, Annotated Edition* (New York: McGraw-Hill, 2006).

8. Josh Allan Dykstra, *Igniting the Invisible Tribe: Designing and Organization that Doesn't Suck* (Silver Thread Publishing, 2012).

9. "Sense of Agency," *Wikipedia, the Free Encyclopedia,* http://en.wikipedia.org/wiki/Sense_of_agency (accessed December 20, 2014).

10. Jamie Notter, *Generational Diversity in the Workplace: Hype Won't Get You Results* (Washington, DC: Culture That Works LLC, 2007) http://www.culturethatworks.net/collections/generations/products/generational-diversity-in-the-workplace-hype-won-t-get-you-results

11. Steve Borsch, *Rise of the Internet Culture* (Eden Prairie, MN: Marketing Directions, Incorporated, 2006), 6.

12. Borsch, 6.

13. Daniel H. Pink, *A Whole New Mind: Moving from the Information Age to the Conceptual Age,* (New York: Riverhead Books, 2005), 33.

14. Pink, *A Whole New Mind,* 33.

15. "Fact Sheet," *Self Storage Association,* http://www.selfstorage.org/ssa/content/navigationmenu/aboutssa/factsheet/ (accessed December 20, 2014).

16. "Women in the United States House of Representatives," *Wikipedia, the Free Encyclopedia,* http://en.wikipedia.org/wiki/Women_in_the_United_States_House_of_Representatives (accessed December 20, 2014).

17. Neil Howe and Reena Nadler, *Millennials in the Workplace: Human Resource Strategies for a New Generation* (Lifecourse Associates, 2010).

18. Brad Stone, "The Secrets of Bezos: How Amazon Became the Everything Store," *Bloomberg BusinessWeek,* October 10, 2013, http://www.businessweek.com/articles/2013-10-10/jeff-bezos-and-the-age-of-amazon-excerpt-from-the-everything-store-by-brad-stone#p1 (accessed December 20, 2014).

19. Brad Stone, "The Secrets of Bezos."

20. George Westerman, Didier Bonnet, and Andrew McAfee. *Leading Digital: Turning Technology into Business Transformation* (Boston: Harvard Business Review Press, 2014), 40.

21. David F. Carr, "TD Bank's Social Strategy: Start Small, Think Big," *InformationWeek*, http://www.informationweek.com/enterprise/td-banks-social-strategy-start-small-think-big/d/d-id/1102358 (accessed December 20, 2014).

22. Ric Dragon, "The Big Brand Theory: TD Bank's Social Customer Service," *Social Media Today*, http://www.socialmediatoday.com/content/big-brand-theory-td-banks-social-customer-service (accessed December 20, 2014).

23. Harrison Coerver and Mary Byers, *Race for Relevance: 5 Radical Changes for Associations* (Washington, DC: ASAE, 2011), 130.

24. Westerman, Bonnet, and McAfee. *Leading Digital*, 20.

25. Notter and Grant, *Humanize*, 232-238.

26. "Gmail," *Wikipedia, the Free Encyclopedia*, http://en.wikipedia.org/wiki/Gmail (accessed December 20, 2014).

27. Chip Heath and Dan Heath, *Switch: How to Change Things When Change Is Hard* (New York: Crown Business, 2010).

28. Sunil Sadasivan, "Why We Don't Have Technical Interviews for Technical Roles at Buffer," *Medium*, https://medium.com/buffer-posts/why-we-dont-ask-technical-questions-for-technical-interviews-at-buffer-73f8132a8abd (accessed December 20, 2014).

29. Joris Luijke, "Atlassian's Big Experiment with Performance Reviews," *Management Innovation Exchange*, http://www.managementexchange.com/story/atlassians-big-experiment-performance-reviews (accessed December 20, 2014).

30. Reid Hoffman, Ben Casnocha, and Chris Yeh. *The Alliance: Managing Talent in the Networked Age* (Boston: Harvard Business Review Press, 2014), p. 42.

31. "Generation Kill." *Foreign Affairs*, March/April 2013, http://www.foreignaffairs.com/discussions/interviews/generation-kill (accessed December 20, 2014

32. Stanley McChrystal, "The Military Case for Sharing Knowledge," *TED*, http://www.ted.com/talks/stanley_mcchrystal_the_military_case_for_sharing_knowledge/transcript?language=en (accessed December 20, 2014).

33. Notter and Grant, *Humanize*, 160.

34. "Our Story," *Menlo Innovations*, http://www.menloinnovations.com/our-story/ (accessed December 20, 2014).

35. "Pair Programming," *Wikipedia, the Free Encyclopedia*, http://en.wikipedia.org/wiki/Pair_programming (accessed December 20, 2014).

36. Jamie Notter, *Culture that Works: How Getting Serious About Culture Unlocks New Performance* (Washington, DC: Culture That Works LLC, 2013), http://www.culturethatworks.net/products/culture-that-works-ebook.

37. Marcia Blenko, Michael Mankins, and Paul Rogers. *Decide and Deliver: Five Steps to Breakthrough Performance in Your Organization* (Boston: Harvard Business Review Press, 2010).

38. Richard Sheridan, *Joy, Inc.: How We Built a Workplace People Love* (New York: Portfolio/Penguin, 2013).

39. Notter and Grant, *Humanize*, 161.

40. Blenko, Mankins, and Rogers. *Decide and Deliver*, 90.

41. Brian Robertson, "The History of Holacracy®: The Discovery of an Evolutionary Algorithm," *Medium*, https://medium.com/about-holacracy/history-of-holacracy-c7a8489f8eca (accessed December 20, 2014).

42. Robertson, "The History of Holacracy®."

43. "How Medium is Building a New Kind of Company With No Managers," *First Round Review*, http://firstround.com/article/How-Medium-is-building-a-new-kind-of-company-with-no-managers (accessed December 20, 2014).

44. Gary Hamel, "Why Bureaucracy Must Die," *Fortune*, March 26, 2014, http://fortune.com/2014/03/26/why-bureaucracy-must-die/ (accessed December 20, 2014).

45. Robert I. Sutton and Huggy Rao, *Scaling Up Excellence: Getting to More Without Settling for Less* (New York: Crown Business, 2014), 108.

46. Clay Shirky, *Here Comes Everybody: The Power of Organizing Without Organizations* (New York: Penguin Books, 2009), 37.

47. Leigh Buchanan, "One Company's Audacious Org Chart: 400 Leaders, 0 Bosses," *Inc.*, April 18, 2013, http://www.inc.com/audacious-companies/leigh-buchanan/morning-star.html (accessed December 20, 2014).

48. Gary Hamel, "First, Let's Fire All the Managers," *Harvard Business Review*, December 2011, https://hbr.org/2011/12/first-lets-fire-all-the-managers/ar/1 (accessed December 20, 2014).

49. Paul Zak, "Managing Without Managers," *Drucker Institute*, February 6, 2012, http://www.druckerinstitute.com/2012/02/managing-without-managers/ (accessed December 20, 2014).

50. Kim Hoogeveen, *Mindset LLC*, http://www.gomindset.com (accessed December 20, 2014).

51. Patrick Lencioni, *The Five Dysfunctions of a Team: A Leadership Fable* (San Francisco: Jossey-Bass, 2002).

52. Jamie Notter, *Better Conflict Conversations: Basic Tools for Managing Conflict in the Workplace* (Washington, DC: Culture That Works LLC, 2013), http://www.culturethatworks.net/products/better-conflict-conversations-tools (accessed December 20, 2014).

53. Bronnie Ware, "Regrets of the Dying," *Bronnie Ware,* http://bronnieware.com/regrets-of-the-dying/ (accessed December 20, 2014).

54. Joe Gerstandt, "Authenticity (and a New Video)," *Joe Gerstandt,* May 2, 2013, http://www.joegerstandt.com/2013/05/authenticity-and-a-new-video/ (accessed December 20, 2014).

55. Jamie Notter, *Making Performance Management Work* (Washington, DC: Culture That Works LLC, 2013), http://www.culturethatworks.net/collections/culture/products/making-performance-management-work (accessed December 20, 2014).

56. Stephen M.R. Covey and Rebecca R. Merrill, *The Speed of Trust: The One Thing That Changes Everything* (New York: Free Press, 2006), 15.

57. W. Chan Kim and Renée Mauborgne, *Blue Ocean Strategy: How to Create Uncontested Market Space and Make the Competition Irrelevant* (Boston: Harvard Business School Press, 2005).

58. W. Chan Kim and Renée Mauborgne, "Blue Ocean Leadership," *Harvard Business Review,* May 2014, 60-72.

59. Franke and Kaul, "The Hawthorne experiments," 623-43.

60. "Merriam-Webster Announces 'Culture'" as 2014 Word of the Year," *Merriam-Webster,* December 15, 2014, http://www.merriam-webster.com/info/2014-word-of-the-year.htm (accessed December 26, 2014).

Acknowledgements

Writing a book is a team sport. Thanks to the following people for the important roles they played:

- Elizabeth Marshall, for shepherding us through this process with great skill and patience.
- Rohit Bhargava, for figuring out how to do business-book publishing right;
- Joe Rominiecki, for exceptional editing.
- Joe Gerstandt, Sandra Giarde, Bryan Kelly, Jason Lauritsen, Amith Nagarajan, Luke Sinclair, and John Stepper for reviewing our manuscript and giving us great feedback.
- Tim Green and Kelly Vlach from Face Out Studio for the best book cover ever.
- Rob Kalnitz and the IdeaPress team for making the book look as good as it does.
- All the organizations who allowed us to interview them or visit them as part of our research, in particular American Society for Surgery of the Hand, Back to the Roots, Happy State Bank, Menlo Innovations, and Quality Living, Inc. Specifically Mark Anderson, Nikhil Arora, Arjun Arora, Pat Hickman, Kayla Carpenter, Rich Sheridan, Anna Flynn, Stephanie Roob, and Jon Pearson for setting everything up and taking such good care of us.
- Kare Anderson, Joe Gerstandt, and Mary Lange, for being the critical connectors to several of those case studies.
- All the Millennials who completed our online survey/interview.
- Our friends and family who put up with all this book writing business, maybe even when we were supposed to be on vacation.
- All of our awesome clients at Culture That Works, who believe in what we do, and our future clients, who will join a tribe that understands why we're so optimistic about the future of business.

Thank you all.

:)

Index

How aligned is your organization with the Millennial generation?

Take the Millennial Alignment Scan

We have created a quick survey you can run with your employees that will give you detailed metrics on how aligned you are with the 4 capacities identified in this book (digital, clear, fluid, and fast).

Through a partnership with the online survey company, QuestionPro, we are now offering our full Millennial Alignment Scan through a powerful digital survey tool that allows you to easily (and economically) gather ongoing intelligence from your workforce.

Sign up today at
http://workxo.questionpro.com

and start building an organization that makes sense in the Millennial era (use referral code WMTO at checkout for a discounted rate).

For more information on our other programs to help organizations create stronger cultures (including the Workplace Genome™ Project), visit www.workxo.com.